IF THE SHOE FITS, GO BAREFOOT

Sofia A. Wellman

This book is dedicated to
Barry Bowman and Shirley Chambers.

While everyone in our life teaches us something,
Barry and Shirley taught me to believe in myself. Thank you.

In loving memory of my mother,
Mary Wellman, who taught me what love is.

CONTENTS

IT'S JUST THE ANGELS

The content of this book evolved through a self-searching process that began with a child's curiosity about the meaning of life. Determined to figure out what life was about, I questioned everything, hoping the meaning of life would be revealed in the answer, yet the answers to my questions only intensified the quest. For instance, I felt frustrated when I was told things such as rain was the result of angels in heaven watering flowers; lightning occurred when the angels were playing a game where they turned their lights on and off; and, of course, thunder was noise from their bowling match. The incompatibilities in what was meant to explain life were apparent to me even when I was a child. I didn't get it. If angels were supposed to protect me, why did they want to scare me and flood our basement in the process?

My sisters went to Sunday school. The day I was old enough to attend couldn't come soon enough. I heard that in Sunday school you learned about God. I just knew all the questions I had about life would be answered there. After all, God knew everything, kind of like Santa Claus did, but more. I saw my Sunday school teacher as the gatekeeper to higher knowledge. Finally I could find the missing pieces to complete the puzzle of life. As soon as I realized she actually believed Noah fit two of each animal on a boat, my enthusiasm dimmed. In fact, most of the stories she told us made no sense at all. I found no meaningful answers there. Sunday school turned out to be nothing more to me than a layover before we were permitted to join the adults at the end of the church service.

A neighbor friend died from a malignant tumor in her eye. Her brother gazed up at the sky and said she was watching over us. I looked up and saw nothing but clouds. After her death, I became sick to my stomach and unable to keep any food down. The doctor told my mother the infliction was caused by my friend's death. I didn't understand. Did I catch her illness?

Life didn't make sense to me, and I didn't feel that I had any ally in figuring life out. Appeased by contradicting, superficial answers, others didn't appear to care if life made sense. That's when I concluded something was wrong with me. I stopped trying to make sense of it all and hitched my wagon to the caravan of survival, where I became distracted with daily living like everyone else. Consumed by the busyness of life, I didn't have time to feel like the misfit who was beamed down on planet earth from a faraway place. Being lost in the confusion didn't feel bad anymore, because I wasn't there alone. Fitting in became more important than understanding existence. I gave in to becoming part of the herd, out of fear of feeling lost all by myself.

Thirty-six years into the life experience, I figured out this "life thing." I built a successful business, and anything I wanted was within arm's reach. The world was my oyster. Outer success saved a seat for me in the big world. I found my purpose. That's when life was all too happy to put the spotlight back on the fact that I hadn't a clue about its meaning, much less my purpose.

In 1996 I was diagnosed with non-Hodgkin's lymphoma. I wish I could say being diagnosed with cancer was the only life-threatening struggle that had to occur to get my attention, but it wasn't. In the following years after cancer, the wake-up calls continued. My resistance to waking up, like hitting the snooze button on an alarm clock, served only as a brief delay from the next jarring moment.

There is nothing like a few brushes with death to make you become majestically aware of the fallacy of immortality. When I was forced to face the end of my life, all my other fallacies tumbled down under the weight of death, like dominoes falling one after the other. All my goals for success were not as seductive, and fitting in was not enough.

I mastered the dance of three steps forward in a search for life's meaning and two steps back into denial, when the task overwhelmed me. The form my denial took was the belief that I didn't need more than business success. The back-and-forth dance exhausted me, since it kept me stuck in the same place, dealing with one personal catastrophe after another.

Life is relentless when we miss the point it wants us to get. Feeling backed against a wall, finally I surrendered. That's when I became determined more than ever to find the meaning of life, even if my motive was like the plea bargaining of an accused felon right before sentencing. I wanted nothing more than to be free from the unavoidable, dramatic events that showed up each year. With my willingness to do whatever it took, my journey began.

New Age concepts were popular, and I read or was told things like, "You create your own existence." What did that mean? Why was I creating hell on earth? Another response was "Life is an illusion." Those chemotherapy treatments felt pretty darned real to me. I particularly liked this epithet: "The universe will give you what you ask for." The most frustrating part about that aphorism was that I asked the universe, God, and any other formless entity, including the archangels, to bring me a loving relationship. I even offered a list of the qualities I wanted my love interest to have, yet the relationships that came into my life quickly transformed from loving to unloving. With clichés that idealize the unreachable, it's no wonder people give up the search. It seemed futile to believe life could make any sense from those concepts floating around. I went from the childhood conclusion that something was wrong with me to an adult variation alternating between "I am pretty darned stupid, because I haven't a clue how to stop all the negative experiences that are occurring" and "Life is really against me."

At one point I became involved in a spiritual community. Believing I was with fellow seekers, I thought I finally found a place where I had allies. Finding meaning to life, which was the need that brought us together, however, became secondary to the primary need we couldn't escape. The primary need was the need to belong. We transferred feeling misaligned with the masses to fitting in with a group searching for answers. As with any need, to assuage a need means a sacrifice of something more valuable, so once again, to fit in, I sacrificed my search for meaning.

The group was overshadowed by the authority of its founder. The range of focus through someone else's lens is too narrow, because it eliminates most of who we are, similar to a camera lens zooming onto a point where nothing else is present but one small part of the whole scene. A limited focus is detrimental, when dealing with people's life. When one adult or group has authority and control over others, the result is people filled with self-judgment, because they are constantly measuring themselves against what they aren't, even if the arrangement appears helpful on the surface.

The quandary in our inherent nature is a search for meaning in life, but the massiveness of the quest makes it feel like we can never find it on our own. As a result, we fall prey to a mirage in an attempt to quench our thirst. Like the person lost in the desert without water who suddenly sees a bubbling stream, we create our own optical illusion when we believe someone else has what we need to give our life meaning.

My experience with a spiritual community is a mere reflection of countless groups, teachings, relationships, and families where the unspoken price of membership is the sacrifice of individuality. Searching for something to give meaning to the chaos, people hand over their lives to a person, group, or cult. They believe they need him/her/them, for their lives to make sense, because they don't believe they can find meaning on their own. It is not the mirage we fall for, but the realization of the mirage that brings us closer to what is real. Nothing can give us meaning but the metaphorical walk across the desert without being betrayed by a mirage. Up until that point, our journey through life is insidious. With unwavering conviction, we remain convinced that the mirage adds value to life, even as our experiences in life exhibit contrary messages. It was no easier for me to give up the mirage of finding meaning through a spiritual guru than it was to give up the mirage of society's ideal of success.

"Each man must look to himself to teach him the meaning of life. It is not something discovered: it is something molded," said Antoine de Saint-Expupery.

An inner perspective is the path carved out, not only from your experiences, but also from what those experiences mean to you. The meaning of life is found only through the jurisdiction of your own inner authority. Any influence that takes you away from yourself is darkness in varying degrees.

Since darkness often comes in the disguise of a colorful illusion too beautiful to resist, people often fall upon darkness in an attempt to find a guiding light. For instance, there is no doubt that Hitler was darkness, yet people followed his authority, not because they were bad people, but because they wanted to be spared the lone journey we must all take. The journey is not an expedition, which is why it begins with facing our aloneness. Darkness is not something remote and isolated to the obvious likeness of Hitler; it is anything that overshadows our inner light.

This book shows you how to magnify the light of your inner authority by helping you understand who you are. Knowing ourselves is the only path to reach our potential as human beings; otherwise our purpose here remains untapped. Life is a series of passages. The most pronounced are birth and death. Birth is the passage from Spirit into form, and death is the passage from form back to Spirit. More significant than those passages is when we are in form and connect with our Spirit. Just like birth and death, it is a passage that must be taken alone. When we understand who we are, what we think we want suddenly becomes insignificant.

IN THE BEGINNING

In the beginning God created the heaven and earth. And the earth was without form, and void; and the darkness was upon the face of the deep. And the spirit of God moved upon the face of the waters. And God said, let there be light: and there was light.

—Genesis 1:1-3

What does that Bible verse mean? The abstract is the esoteric world that lends meaning to the essence of who we are. It explains the inner world that our sense of sight, smell, hearing, and touch outline. Our natural inclination is to define the abstract with the physical outline we intellectually comprehend. Mythologies are created every time we try to explain the inner world. Taken literally, mythologies lose their impact. Those stories are the form through which energy is conveyed to a deeper part of us. That energy is fuel for the level of consciousness often referred to as our soul. While words are a vehicle through which the intent of energy can be delivered, before we know it, we are stuck on the words, and the potential impact of the energy on our soul is spoiled. If we have too much energy to absorb for day-to-day living, drama is the byproduct of that higher energy dispersed through our personality.

We're not comfortable containing energy, because we don't understand the need for it beyond physical functioning. During a museum exhibit just the other day, I saw a painting that stirred something deep inside of me, and I quickly pushed the surge of energy into the outer world. I described the painting's colors and textures and continued remarking to my friend how the painting resembled the physical likeness of what it captured. Many things can have a powerful effect on us, such as a story, poem, conversation, or song, often when the words themselves don't justify the impact. We may brush against the awareness that somehow we touched into another level and then quickly direct our mind to something tangible or relational to something outside of us. The inner stirring created is the impact when energy touches on another level of our existence. Sparked by the inspirational energy, the level defined as soul level consciousness is awakened and nurtured. From that level, we create from a place of knowing, commonly referred to as intuition. Creating from an inner impulse is not limited to art; it can be a business idea, a solution to a problem, some awareness about ourselves, and so on.

Because everyone has had different experiences in life, based on those experiences, life is rendered differently. I have seen three or more people involved in a situation that each defined as if describing a different event. I used to believe all but one was lying. The process of interpretation certainly keeps gossip alive and the legal system busy, and it is the precursor of most arguments, yet to use the energy behind any experience in a way befitting our destiny, it has to mean something different for each of us.

To one man a car accident can catapult him into feeling more gratitude for life; to another, it can unleash pent-up anger that needs to clear before he feels empowered enough to meet his potential. The energy absorbed from any experience is more important than the details of the physical process. While the description of an event is the outline of what occurred, it can never accurately define what really happened, because the essence of the experience is unique to each person. In the past, if I had an interesting conversation with someone, I would try to replay the words of the conversation in my mind. Now I know that the actual words are less meaningful than the impact of energy exchanged. Words do not convey our intent; the energy behind the words exchanges more information.

Whether or not you intellectually comprehend this book is less important than the experience of being receptive to the energy behind the written words. Although some words are likely to bring your attention down to the word itself, seemingly as sudden and startling as a jolt caused by the change in the pavement during a leisurely walk, it happens because those words carry a lot of emotional energy collectively and individually. I will provide the key to the files I have on the words most likely to cause a tangle with the energy behind their intent. For example, one word guaranteed to illicit a strong opinion is *God*. For one person, the meaning of God points to the East; to another it may point to the South, and so on. I will hand you the files for those words. I am not asking you to rearrange the files in your mind, but to borrow mine, so the flow of energy does not feed a knot of conflict. Often our defenses cause us to run circles in our mind, changing nothing other than leaving us more exhausted.

When I walk my puppy past a neighbor's house where a basset hound is contained by an electric fence, my puppy runs circles around the dog while the hound lies there acting as if she were a fly he can't be bothered to shoo away. Although the other dog doesn't twitch a muscle, my dog thinks they are interacting the whole time, and while nothing changes on his end from the moment she ran up to him, she walks away panting and exhausted. Our defenses are like a young dog that can't resist the impulse to interact with what is in front of her. They leave us exhausted, even when we have changed nothing, gained no new insight, or not impacted another.

Since learning evolves as we do, a single revelation will not lead us to enlightenment, but illuminates more of who we are along the way. Even someone as brilliant as Carl Jung, a master at understanding the psyche, said we have to take what he brought forth and evolve it further, based on our developing awareness. There is not an absolute truth, but an unfolding of truth that correlates with the unfolding of ourselves. We stop learning when we believe we have found truth.

Learning is absorbed from various angles. Where something may be the catalyst to bring what we needed to learn to our attention, the process of learning is cyclical. For instance, a life lesson typically comes with one theme that our experiences revolve around for a while until we get the message, and then we move on to the next lesson.

To learn something at a level that creates change, we must hear it more than four thousand times, according to Buddha. The people this book affects will have heard or experienced what I have written somehow, some way, something like three thousand, nine hundred and ninety-nine times before. Therefore, if I awaken you to yourself, I should be revered no more than the alarm clock that awakens you in the morning. We take in what we need when we are ready, and there are myriad ways to find what we need. If I had not written this book, you would have found what it meant to you elsewhere.

Perhaps you will vehemently disagree with what I write, in which case I ask you to go beyond your judgment. You will learn more about yourself by understanding the reason you need to deflect what you are reading. I did not write this book to make you feel good about where you are in life. I wrote it to spotlight the places where you are imprisoned. We possess the key, but cannot open the door to the iron gate without seeing the location of the lock that holds it shut.

When I think of how people perceive information, it reminds me of how I am received on the bike path. It is considerate to announce "On your left," when you are about to pass people, so they don't unwittingly cut in front of you and cause an accident. Some people give a nod, acknowledging the warning, almost as a thank-you. Then there are those who get irritated and find the warning annoying. They don't connect it to its purpose, to prevent a disaster. I find most bewildering the reactions from the people who get downright aggressive and spout off profanity or give crude hand gestures. One elderly woman raised her cane as though ready to knock me off my bike. Those folks use my helpfulness as something to fight against, giving their anger an outlet. Worse than misdirecting their anger, they can't see beyond it, and in the process neglect themselves and invite danger.

You may be tempted to skip ahead to a chapter that calls to you, but because each chapter builds on the prior chapters, keep to the order I purposely laid out, beginning with "the files" below. As you read these files, keep in mind it is the least relational part of the book. It may feel similar to reading the directions to assemble a product, where the pieces don't seem to fit the directions. Don't allow yourself to become frustrated with this chapter; there is no product to assemble. If you can't intellectually connect these files with the files in your mind, remember you are borrowing these files to read the book. With that in mind, you will get what you need.

God, defined by religion, is often personified as an ancient man, distinguished by a long white beard, who sits on clouds in heaven. God is interpreted as the guiding force behind the universe we are part of, as well as our individual world. In metaphysical terms, the words *the universe* are used to illicit the same guiding force, but rather than being identified with a person, it is identified with a dynamic collective energy. In mysticism, God is defined as a force that enlivens everything in existence and is synonymously referred to as "Spirit, life-force, and divinity," which are all the words you will see throughout my book to depict the life-force in everything, including each of us individually. Rather than signifying it as a guiding force, I will depict it as a patterned force seeking its most compatible form. For instance, the roses in my yard continue to bloom as roses. Every year since I had them planted more than ten years ago, I can expect roses throughout the year. Never once have they bloomed to look like the azaleas planted close by.

While the pattern force is evident in the form everything takes and is perceivable through our physical senses, on an inner level, that patterned force is the impetus that keeps life in motion. As human beings we spend our life seeking the most compatible form of experience for the Spirit, life-force, divinity, or God as it comes through us, thus making us co-creators with the higher energy. Failure to align ourselves with the experiences that are the most compatible form creates disharmony in our lives. How and why we misalign our energy is the crux of this book.

Consciousness is another word with many meanings. If you will conceptualize God, Spirit, life-force, and divinity as I have defined it, as a force, if you want to use that force, it must be activated by something. Because a force is dynamic, just like the force of electricity, it cannot be contained in a stagnant state. The best analogy to define consciousness came to me while I was discussing vaccinating my dog with her vet. In effort to help me understand the vaccination process in simple terms, the vet told me that an adjuvant is a chemical that carries viral vaccination into the dog's system. Unless the virus is carried in an adjuvant, the dog's immune system could destroy the virus, nullifying the immune-building properties of the vaccine. Consciousness, like an adjuvant, is the vehicle by which we bring the force of Spirit into the manifested world; however, unlike the virus destroyed by the dog's immune system without the adjuvant, the pure force of Spirit would destroy our physical self, if consciousness did not act as its activating vehicle. As we expand in consciousness, we can access more power from our Spirit, since we have a larger container to hold that energy. Where we contract in consciousness, we cause disharmony, because the energy empowers our emotions instead, which is why, once we begin to expand consciousness, turning back to ignorance is even more harmful.

Awareness is said to be the vibratory frequency of consciousness. If a baby cries every time he needs something, he becomes aware that when he cries, his need will be met, be it the need for a fresh diaper, food, or pain relief. At some point we realized crying was no longer the most effective way to get our needs met, and we negotiated other means. While it is important to apply awareness into the daily living experience, the application of awareness into physical life is not how we expand consciousness. We also have to apply what we learned from our experiences into understanding ourselves. Believing that our Spirit permeates consciousness is not enough. Until we prioritize the application of awareness to understand that patterned force of our Spirit, we are not fully applying ourselves in life. When we are willing to exchange the comfort of what we have been taught to understand who we are, we are poised to use awareness to expand consciousness. It is not what we intellectually grasp, but the application of that awareness that is key.

Someone with high awareness doesn't necessarily live from a higher level of consciousness. Like a mountain climber has a more expansive view the higher she climbs, a higher level of awareness allows us to comprehend life from a perspective that encompasses more, but it is our choice how we apply it. Similarly, the mountain climber has a choice how she uses the experience from her climb. She can use it to challenge the climbers on their way to the summit by throwing rocks down; she can boast on her Facebook page about her trials and tribulations to make it to the summit; or she can internalize the energy from the experience where she is deeply touched by the beauty and more in touch with herself for having done it. With each challenge on the assent, she learned more about her fears, her weaknesses, her strengths and who she was. The same woman returned to her day-to-day life feeling empowered enough to have the courage to go back to school, get her master's in psychology, and afterwards go on to teach, write, and counsel, where she has a positive influence on others.

We project only about ten percent of consciousness through our physical body and its tool, the brain. The ten percent is quoted as scientific fact, though scientists still believe the brain holds the other ninety percent someplace locked away from their grasp. They continue to examine the brain in search for the other ninety percent that we haven't tapped into. Since the rest of consciousness is not in our brain, it will never be found there, no matter how smart the scientists conducting the research. The other ninety percent is not contained in physical form, and while it is unconscious to us at the physical level, it has the most impact on our life. It is that ninety percent that is the primary focus of this book.

When it is said we are "mind beings," we are not referring to the brain or the use of the intellect demonstrated by the brain. Consider the mind and the brain as distinctly different as the carpenter from the hammer he uses. As the carpenter uses the hammer for a tool, so do we use our brain. *Mind* is a word that I will use interchangeably with consciousness, soul, and man, all to mean the same thing. It is the non-physical inner terrain where the mysterious ninety percent can be found.

The terms *child*, *teenager*, and *adult* label the developmental stages of our physical body, as they can mark the growth of consciousness. If consciousness had a physical body, we would see the body become larger, stronger, and more developed over time. Unlike the physical body that is nurtured through the assimilation of food, consciousness is nurtured by assimilating experiences, which is precisely the reason why sitting on a mountain and meditating for a year will not grow consciousness in the same way as our day-to-day life experiences can. Even the experiences that seem in hindsight to be the result of poor decisions, depending on how we integrate them into our life, can nurture consciousness.

We use consciousness through four levels of our being. The physical level is where we literally manifest into the physical world. For example, I physically wrote a book by typing into the computer combinations of letters that formed combinations of words, but the idea to write a book did not come from the physical level. Where did it originate? It came from the formative level, which is the level quantum physics defines as particles and waves, where matter is formed. I will also refer to the formative level as the level of intellect and desire. I physically typed letters into my computer, but they were not random letters that formed words by chance. I formed my thoughts into words using my intellect. From a strong desire to help others, I kept at it until I was finished. While my intellect was able to form words from my thoughts, my desire was what motivated me to write each day instead of making money, watching television, or doing something else. Where did the raw material for my intellect and the motivation to write originate? The creative level is the liaison between our spiritual level and our formative level. It is the raw material for the formative level and contains the pattern of our spiritual expression, the same pattern the rose bush follows when it blooms roses, rather than azaleas. With self-will we are not quite as obedient to the pattern that complies with the expressive, patterned, force of our Spirit. The underlying force that permeates our existence, the spiritual level, is the expression we are meant to bring into creation. We are ignited by that spark of God within.

To use an analogy, the breath blown into a trumpet that manifests as the sound we hear is Spirit, life-force, divinity, or the God within. The trumpet is the creative level that holds the pattern the sound flows through. The keys on the trumpet are the formative level that molds the sound, based how we have learned to play, and the actual sound we hear reaches the physical level.

The terms *man* and *mankind* are used to simplify into two levels the above four levels through which we exist. "Man is made in the image and likeness of God," as it combines the spiritual and creative levels. Mankind is the fraction of consciousness that infiltrates our physical body, but it is not limited to the physical body, as it is tangible. It encompasses our senses as well as our intellect and emotions. Mankind combines the formative and physical levels. Like the parent who tries to impress on his child the formula for right living, man tries to impress onto mankind a patterned force. Mankind is the delivery agent man uses to bring heaven to earth. How we hit the keys on the trumpet determines if the physical sound is in or out of harmony. In life, we, too, make choices that determine if we experience living in or out of harmony.

Man is eternal and experiences the continuity of life through reincarnation. Only the vehicle dies, the physical body. Man builds a new vehicle based on karma and is magnetically drawn to the appropriate life environment based on the same.

If what you just read is as clear as mud, you are ready to continue. Remember, the terminology defines the name for the files, but it is not the essence of the content.

WHERE IS THE HOLY GRAIL?

For the past six years, I have been making a documentary on death. Three years into the process, I flew to California to interview a woman who is trying to comprehend an enormous amount of loss. Less than a year had passed since she and her family planned and saved to take a vacation she described as wonderful. Their return flight was late, which complicated the coordination of the car service that was supposed to meet them. Once they coordinated with the driver, negotiated luggage, and were on their way home, she text messaged her sister to let her know she and her family made it home safely. She then called the brother they left, to relay the same message. Minutes later her driver's path was crossed by a man too drunk to be behind the wheel of a car. The woman's twenty-one-year-old daughter, fourteen-year-old son, and two-year-old grandson were killed in the accident. Her husband was left with brain damage. Only she and her son-in-law survived intact. Even the driver of the car service was killed.

I had the opportunity to spend two days with her while she re-lived what happened and how she was coping in the aftermath. While I interviewed her for my film, I asked, "What did you learn from the experience?"

She answered, "I don't know. I know there is something I am supposed to learn. I am not sure what it is yet, but I know in the appropriate time, it will be revealed to me."

After working out at the gym one evening, I went into the whirl-pool to relax. A woman I never met joined me and apparently decided I needed to hear all of her problems. Determined to share the drama of her life, she seemed most caught up in the divorce she went through two years before. I wanted to break her stride down the path of the honorary victim, which she seemed all too comfortable taking, so I asked her, "What did you learn from your experience?"

She pondered for a moment, and then without hesitation said, "I learned that men are horrible."

In the first example, we observe someone taking the pieces from a life shattered and absorbing the truth as it reveals itself, no matter how painful the process, whereas in the second example, the woman is not absorbing anything and is actually deflecting each and every particle of truth her experience offers.

Just as the cells of our physical body assimilate nutrients from the food we ingest after it is broken down into molecules and particles that can be absorbed, often our most devastating experiences can be the catalyst to break down our life so that we can assimilate the nutrient of truth. There is beauty in the breakdown, because in the breakdown, fate hands us clues to answers for the questions we otherwise stay too busy to ask. It is up to us whether we are receptive to our truth or choose to deflect truth by wrapping it in blame.

In my life, pain has been my greatest motivator, sending me on a quest for answers. I have often felt like a knight on a crusade searching for the Holy Grail. The Holy Grail has been symbolically endowed with the answers to everything. Mythology shares the search for this sacred chalice through stories of its origin, subsequent disappearance, and possible sightings throughout history. It has been connected to the sacred chalice Jesus and his disciples drank from during the last supper, which is replicated by many religions during the transubstantiation, where the bread and wine are turned into the body and blood of Christ. As quoted in Matthew 26:28, during the last supper, Jesus said, "For this is my blood of the new testament, which is shed for many for the remission of sins." Symbolically it can be said through the blood of our experiences, we are forgiven the ignorance that causes us the greatest difficulties, because we have learned.

Interestingly, the chronicle of the original story was never completed. The legend of this sacred chalice has been rewritten and redefined throughout time. The story is an allegory of life. As the Holy Grail parallels our endless individual search for meaning, it would need to be rewritten and redefined over time.

No matter how the story is told, though, the focus is always on a long and arduous journey to find the Holy Grail. Though the

23

adventure to find truth may be different for each seeker, the impact of the journey will be greater than the meaning the seeker initially sought. In our search to discover the meaning of life, we will find more than intellectual understanding, which appears to be the purpose behind the pursuit.

I have found knowledge far greater than that of the intellect. Believing that I was on a quest for a tangible truth, I was surprised to find that truth is anything but tangible, much less finite. Through our experiences, we build an inner vessel to contain the wisdom of our Spirit, a vessel similar to the Holy Grail, represented as a chalice. It is a sacred chalice built from truth that far exceeds the intellect. In one of the written accounts of the Holy Grail, when the seeker touched it, he was killed. Similarly, the power of our Spirit is ruthless without the inner containment of truth.

In effect our experiences in life provide the material we use to construct our inner chalice. Each experience has the potential to expand our inner chalice, because the essence found within our experience allows us to deepen our understanding of ourself. As our self-mastery strengthens, so does the ability to contain the knowing of our Spirit. Our ability to contain that power is relative to our ability to interpret the lesson from our experience as it applies to us individually.

I didn't need an astrology chart to tell me one of my biggest challenges was going to be love relationships. Long before the explanation given to me for all the lines crossing over each other in one quadrant on my birth chart, I was aware that love relationships were not my boon in life. Since I didn't have any awareness about the inner workings of attraction, I assumed it was a numbers game, and in time the right person would come along. When the numbers exceeded my generous allowance for practice, I felt life was unfair to me. Only then did I realize the heartache from love gone bad was my admission ticket to learn about myself. For each of us the ticket is different, but when pain and anger burn off, a delicate mass of strength is left behind, and we are brave enough to trek the inward journey as a way to heal. The seemingly unfair debit is balanced by the credit from wisdom gained.

Like with the sacred chalice, the truth did not lie in the object, but in the answers from the experiences. The gift is the peace that surpasses understanding, since it is made from the substance of inner knowing, often described as straight-knowledge, intuition, or our inner voice. For instance, I learned far more about myself when I was able to honestly access why I joined a spiritual group, how I interacted in it, and why it was difficult for me to leave, than I did from its teachings, which were supposed to bring me to self-realization.

Unlike gifts received at Christmastime, the Holy Grail is not bestowed upon its recipient. Unlike the lottery, it is not won by chance. It is the reward of increasing our awareness by observing and learning from life experiences each and every day without judgment. It is the result of hard work and the discipline to look within for the meaning from what we perceive as failure.

Some time ago, the beginning of this book was lost because of my inability to save the material correctly onto the hard drive of the computer. Rather than sulking about it, I decided that the message in that experience was to start over. Perhaps my original beginning was not what the book needed. We must observe the messages in our reality that come through not only our experiences, but also through our interaction with things like a computer and the people surrounding us. These things are clues to help us know who we are. When we accept our experiences as a reflection of an inner situation we need to become conscious about, there is nothing to fear.

Symbolic as a reflection of us, one of two things can be garnered from what seems to be occurring *to us* on the outside. First, what we think we want and the purpose of our Spirit are out of sync. Mankind's creation is not in sync with man's expression. We may create what we think we want, and then our Spirit is sure to bring forth the events that show what we thought we wanted doesn't fit the expression of our Spirit. Unless we've been ignoring the previous messages, a lesson usually doesn't come in one fell swoop. If we can recognize an explosive situation as a karmic debt accumulating from our resistance to learn over lifetimes, it is not an injustice to us in this life, but a chance to redirect our life.

In school when I missed a question on a test, it was always more important to me to know the right answer. I had an innate curiosity that often got me in trouble, because I refused to move on until I understood the concept. Memorizing the right answer for the next test was not enough. Often I felt left behind. The teachers and parents seemed more concerned about the fact that I missed a question, than whether I learned the correct answer. In life, I find the opposite to be true. I get left behind when I don't bother to understand the meaning of what is occurring in my reality. Usually, whatever "it" is will continue to occur until I not only comprehend the correct meaning of the message, but also implement what I learned.

There are also events that exercise our new strength. As we grow in awareness, that awareness is tested. It must be grounded into manifestation. We may think we have further developed a principle inside of us, such as patience, but until we are tested on patience, we don't actually know how thoroughly we have developed the attribute of patience. When someone cuts us off in traffic, we may quickly find we have not acquired true patience.

Even if we integrate the understanding from our experiences on one level, we are tested again wherever the stakes for failing are more significant. Whereas in school, passing a test with a high score was celebratory, passing a test in life means you don't even realize you are taking a test. You become oblivious to what was once a hurdle, once you develop the inner principle to overcome the potential stumbling block.

We may argue the validity of using reality as a symbol. Usually when people get defensive, it is because they interpret the meaning of what is occurring as harsh. There is no need to judge what is showing up in our reality. I'm sure you heard the saying, "Don't shoot the messenger." I would like to modify it by saying, "Don't destroy the message."

I took a friend shopping to ease the angst from her recent breakup. Everywhere she went, she looked for signs to indicate if her decision to end the relationship was right. In one store there was a sign, The Yes Department. Certainly she was relieved. After we ate lunch two hours later, she cracked open her fortune cookie and found out her fortune didn't concur with The Yes Department. She was horrified as she handed me the fortune that read, "You must not act in haste."

Life viewed from the perspective of a snapshot is conclusive, but without the information we need if we are to come to an accurate conclusion. The messages given to us in life are not snapshots, but much like a movie unfolding before us, developing the plot and characters with each scene. All our decisions are correct, because they are the substance for what comes next, which is always what we need, to grow. The messages we pull from our experiences change as we do.

For twenty years, I have handled every facet of real estate, from sales to rentals, as well as construction projects. If you asked me, I'd normally say managing conflict and error is an aspect of what I do for a living. If I paid a subcontractor for a service not rendered correctly, I would not be managing my business well. I deal with things such as a forty-dollar overcharge from a satellite TV company, an overblown plumbing bill, or a lawsuit filed by the man who incorrectly installed his own home theater and still feels righteous enough to sue me for payment for his time.

There was a period in my life when the outer conflict reflected my inner conflict. During a period when I was being catapulted into self-awareness, I struggled to let go of what no longer fit, as I sorted out who I was from who I thought I should be. It was kind of like fighting with yourself while going through your closet and trying to discard what is no longer useful.

The conflicts of managing multiple aspects of real estate haven't magically disappeared, but the difference is in how I handle them. I respond more than I react. I am less attached, and therefore less compulsive about my need for perfection around the outcome. Now when I say, "Conflict is part of my job," I mean it is not part of me. We are the only ones capable of determining what our life is reflecting, because we are the only ones who can see our life with an unobstructed view. Someone looking on the outside in may think my life doesn't look different, because I still deal with conflict.

Evaluating our experiences should be no more complex than gauging our athletic abilities. If I am training to run a marathon, and each day after practice my feet are so sore that I can hardly walk, I could put all my effort into soothing my sore feet, or I could use it as a sign that I need better shoes. If I continue to train and do not progress with the course I have followed, I could consider myself a failure at running or I could research other training methods. I might take the advice of a friend who runs track. If I practice his methods and still see no improvement, I could experiment with other training systems or a combination tailored specifically for me. I may find that running a marathon is not for me, or I may find that I haven't found the training style that best suits me. My conclusion would be based on an assessment of results from my experience over time, as it needs to be with how we evaluate what our life is reflecting to us.

If how we evaluate our experiences is what changes our lives, our experiences themselves are not life changing, which makes me think of MSG, which stands for monosodium glutamate, a chemical compound. A chef who uses MSG can enhance the flavor of a recipe with minimal ingredients. If, for instance, she is making chicken soup, a little MSG can give the soup broth the flavor of a whole chicken, using only half. The most interesting part about MSG is that unlike a spice, it does nothing to change the food it is used with. Instead, it changes how our taste buds perceive the food. Our experiences in life are similar to MSG, in that they don't change our life, but they change how we perceive our life. Pain and sorrow, rightly regarded, will project a different effect in our future. Our growth is dependant upon truth revealed, which is never uncovered before our ability to realize it. We are always given experiences that we have the strength to handle, even if they seem unfathomable at the time.

The bumps and sorrows we encounter along the way aren't there to harm us. They are there to shatter the crystallization of our outdated beliefs and concepts so we can expand our inner chalice. As we surrender to the inner knowing that our chalice is made from, we flow with our Spirit as it fills the chalice or we comprehend the meaning of "Let go and let God."

The quest for the Holy Grail was never described as easy, no matter which author told the story. Likewise, the construction of our inner chalice will never be defined by any of us as easy. The difficulty is not from the search for inner meaning found in our experiences, but because that search usually doesn't begin until we have painfully struggled to search for the answers to life on the outside, to no avail.

RESPONSIBILITY

When the unimaginable becomes part of reality, it is not always inspiring to know anything is possible. A psychologist once told me that the worst day in my life would be when I knew I was not crazy or not going to kill myself. In other words, the day I had to face myself. At the time, I couldn't relate to her statement.

Shortly thereafter, I thought I was crazy. It is a fine line between sanity and insanity. Chemical imbalance is the kinder, gentler term I chose. It was the hand that held my emotional state on the edge of sanity, barely protecting me from falling into the pit of insanity. Logical as I am, I could use my gene pool to reconcile why I was an emotional wreck. My family, as all do, had its quirks. My mother could easily have been labeled a worrier and my father was obsessive-compulsive. Next in line, I had an uncle who was bipolar and an aunt who was psychotic. My neuroses were all sorted out through the family tree, which made it a lot easier to justify how I reacted to what occurred.

Astrologically, it is predicted that everyone goes through a Saturn Return that translates into a life-changing event somewhere between the ages of late twenties and early thirties. Right on schedule at the budding age of thirty, I discovered the person with whom I was in a nine-year relationship was having an affair. In hindsight it would be shortsighted to blame my reaction on the relationship. As we build our life, we construct limits around our fears. Like the bumper that takes the first hit when the car crashes, those limits get jarred when our reality shifts. Our fears get exposed, leaving us more vulnerable than we can tolerate.

The details of the fated day could easily mimic other worst days. The difference about the events of that day is they led me to conclude I was not crazy or going to kill myself. On that day all check points were cleared to launch an endless journey of self-discovery. Had I stayed in that relationship, not only would I have missed many learning experiences that have encouraged me to meet my potential, but I also would have missed the many people I needed to meet, people who influenced my development. Both things have brought me to where I am today. More than two decades later, I see my Spirit could not have been contained comfortably in the safety of the life I thought I wanted. Fortunately I had not known then what was ahead, or I might have died from fright. Life does not get easier, but we certainly become stronger.

The synchronistic events began with a curious but innocent visit to a psychic. It was my first such experience, and I nervously made the forty-five-minute drive by myself in secret. I justified my secret with the excuse that others would think I was foolish for going, but in actuality, I did not want to admit to the trip if I didn't like what he said.

What he told me made no sense at the time. I left thinking the trip was silly and a waste of time and money. Relieved that no one knew, I thought it was easy to put the visit out of my mind, yet what he told me a long time ago is more vivid in my mind than what I did yesterday. He told me that he saw someone named Donna, and that through Donna, my life would open up to amazing opportunities. He saw another woman named Terrie. He wasn't sure what her role was, but said watch for a Terrie. He also saw me heavily involved with the public and people.

I was a manufacturer's representative for a Fortune 500 company. Although I dealt with people, they were set accounts. I couldn't consider my career as being in the public eye. I did well in my position, but I had not felt challenged with my career. I had outgrown my job about nine years before, according to my manager, within the first year of being there. My manager encouraged me to go after a new position, but I didn't think my relationship could handle the relocation or the energy it would take, so without regret, I made the choice to stay complacent.

My life fell apart shortly after my session with the psychic, when my partner had an affair with an acquaintance of ours by the name of Donna. It didn't make sense. How was that experience opening my life up to amazing opportunities? My initial reaction was to run, as if I could get away from the pain. Immediately I put our house on the market, but I contradicted that action as quickly as I took it. I demanded the Realtor price our home twenty percent higher than her recommendation. It was clearly an attempt to hold on to my life as I knew it.

The first person who saw the house bought it at full price. Her name was Terrie. The cycle of time tends to set its stride based on what needs to happen. I can look back on the whirlwind home sale and know if the sale had not happened so fast, it may not have happened at all. Out of fear of the unknown, my partner and I probably would have worked through the affair. In a desperate plea to keep the past from moving into the future, a week before the closing, I called Terrie to ask her if I could buy our home back from her at a higher price than she paid. She said, "No."

What I didn't see was my old life had departed from underneath me before the sale of the house, but the house sale, being symbolic of that finality, was devastating. The closing was similar to a funeral ritual that cements the reality of death.

My old life was like a dam acting as a barricade. Instead of holding back water, it served to hold back everything I had not faced about myself. When the home closing was final, the dam broke and the flood of emotions that I had been holding back became overwhelming. I was forced to face all my sorrow without anything to soften the hard edges of truth. The truth was I hadn't a clue who Sofia Wellman was.

After my significant relationship ended, I could not function. I was not eating, sleeping, or working. While I will never underestimate the enormity of love lost in a world where it is so hard to find, it was apparent from the depth of my reaction that I lost more than a love relationship. I lost the distraction that kept me from myself. Not being able to live with the vulnerability, I constructed new, more apparent distractions. I endured a stream of torturous, obsessive thoughts. From a non-smoker and occasional drinker, I became a chain smoker until I couldn't breathe and drank until I passed out. It was a horrible, ungodly, dark time, and I felt no hope of anything ever being good again.

I checked myself in and out of a psych ward. I couldn't sit still long enough to stay. One minute I was making moccasins during group leather-making class, and the next I was pacing up and down the halls, stopping by the nurses' station to discuss ways in which they could improve the facility. My anxiety was untamable. I felt a reprieve only when I engaged in a phone conversation with friends or family members who gave me a moment of hope about getting my "old" life back. I savored their words when they said things like, "The end isn't written; you two might have just needed a break. You can still get back together." As soon as I hung up the phone, I was miserable again. The only solution I saw was to end my life. Death was the only way I knew to get beyond the torment.

I have always heard that people who choose to end their life do so in revenge. I am here to say revenge was the only thing I didn't feel. I was not blaming anyone else for what was happening. Contrary to what anyone else said, I irrationally believed that I had ruined my life. Blaming another might have been a better bridge to cross than the one of self-loathing I was traversing.

I lived in Cincinnati at the time, and my sister and her husband were on their way to Cincinnati to attend a family function with her in-laws. I knew she would be looking for me, since we were planning to get together when she got there. I worked out of my home, so it would have been a while before my coworkers noticed I was missing. With my twisted logic, I deemed it important for someone to find my dead body quickly. By then I was in a rental house and didn't want to create too much hardship for the owners, so I decided to hang myself with my karate belt before my sister got there. I had been taking karate for about a year and was a proud orange belt. I felt empowered in class. It was ironic that I had chosen to end my life with a symbol that represented empowerment to me. My life was filled with symbols of empowerment that propped me up, masking the disempowerment I felt at my core.

A higher power circumvented the suicide plan. First I got a call from a dear friend of the family checking in on me. After that call, I still felt total despair. My intent was to continue my suicide attempt, and then another close friend called. She sensed I was incoherent, but she lived in Columbus, Ohio, which was a good two hours away. Feeling helpless and not knowing what else to do, she phoned the psychologist I was seeing. An answering machine picked up.

Still, I saw no reason not to continue my suicide plan, though in my final moments I was looking for one. Within minutes after hanging up with my friend, I received a call from the psychic I had seen. He rarely calls people, especially those he barely knows. Even though I had seen him only once, he intuitively was prompted to call me. When I answered, he asked me how I was doing. I told him I was going to kill myself and said it as nonchalantly as the habitual social response, "fine."

He laughed and said, "Get your head out of the electric oven; that won't work. You will only singe your eyelashes." His irreverence to what I thought was my most dismal confession took me off guard. He even found humor in it. We talked for hours, and something sank in. More important than being able to hear him, I began to have hope. That day I began a treacherous climb on the most unstable terrain I had ever walked. The pursuant months were not easy.

A higher power came to my aid that day. I believe the higher power to be my higher self or Spirit; otherwise, I would presume that others who follow through and kill themselves were not "worthy" of being saved. A part of me wasn't ready to leave. That part called to me all the force it could muster to prevent my physical self from leaving prematurely. Consciously it was not I who solicited the aid of those calls in my perceived final moments of life. Ultimately, we do have some say in when we leave, even if it isn't a conscious choice. Years later, a Vedic astrologer from India said I almost left physical life that year. At first I thought his timing was off, because years later, I came close to death several times, but then I remembered that fateful day

Although I did not leave that day through physical death, something inside me did die. A once-comfortable naivety breathed its final breath. Unbeknown to me, since I was the person others could count on, the one who paid all her bills on time, my first lesson in responsibility was born that day.

Egg Whites, Please

I am a slow learner. What appears as stubbornness is an innate desire to understand all there is to know about something. I have often felt like a scientist. I can't just touch on an experience, I have to take it apart and study it from every angle. I become consumed by what holds my attention.

What the psychic said to me on the day I almost committed suicide continues to consume my attention. He said, "Nothing flows from out to in; everything comes from within." No matter how many times I have hidden behind blame, life reminds me—sometimes gently, but often not—it all begins with me. This learning continues to deepen with time, beginning with the intimate connection with myself established on that fateful day in 1991. It was the day when the events of my life dictated that I could no longer look outward, because everything around me, everything defining who I was, crumbled.

In therapy I unraveled the threads of childhood, trying to make sense of the fabric of beliefs that clothed me. On occasion I blamed my childhood for my pain, if the weight of responsibility got too heavy. Usually in those moments there was something about myself I wasn't ready to face. It took a while before I learned the weight of responsibility is lighter than the weight of blame.

Some people blame their childhood, because they believe that's where the patterns that dictate their life were formed. I say we incarnated with those patterns, and childhood is the "holding tank" that preserves them. When we were growing up, my sister had a fish tank. When she added more fish from the store, she had to keep them in their water-filled plastic bag and place the bag into the water-filled aquarium. It gave the fish an incubation period that prepared them to tolerate their new environment. If she let them out too soon, they'd go into shock and die. Like those fish, we were born into the environment that sustained the patterns of where we left off from our last incarnation. It is an incubation period that holds us safely until we are adults.

Examining childhood is an effective way to understand the patterns we brought forward. Just as separating an egg yolk from the egg white is easier before the eggs get scrambled, it is easier to see the patterns that dictate our life from the environment we were born into, but to go back and belabor childhood events, looking for a reason we are the way we are, is how we remain in the holding tank.

One time, my sister accidentally killed her fish when she kept them in the holding tank too long. Their environment, over time, was too confined. Our current incarnation merged with our past, but our potential is the evolution away from the past. The individuation process starts when we become self-responsible. As George Bernard Shaw said, "We are made wise not by the recollection of our past, but by the responsibility for our future."

Wallowing in the past "wrongs" of childhood, we use the future to pay for the past. Once I had dinner with a friend. The service at the restaurant was disappointing and the food was mediocre. For the rest of the evening, long after we finished dining, my friend continued to communicate her disappointment about the restaurant. We had plenty of time to continue the evening differently, but she stayed stuck in her anger about our dining experience, which had long past. In her inability to let go, she continued to pay the bill far beyond what we owed to the restaurant with the remainder of the evening as well as reflection on it years later. The lesson: You have paid for the past; don't use the present to keep paying for it.

It disturbed me when my grade-school history teacher announced that history repeats itself. He said many of the battles fought throughout history carried over and were fought again in the next decade. I was horrified then, but am more horrified now by some of the personal battles I repeat. The saying "History repeats itself" is a reflection of the fact we don't easily move away from the past.

Typically where we struggle with life, we are repeating the same pattern a parent also struggled with. For example, I knew a married couple in a tumultuous relationship heading for divorce. They had a five-year-old daughter. When the wife of the couple was five, her parents' struggling marriage ended in divorce. This experience didn't make her parents responsible for her failing marriage, but provided a pivotal point, where she could choose to blame them or use the information to understand herself. We can change our personal history. Just taking different action from our parents is often the opposite side of the same coin and will procure the same outcome.

Seeds of awareness are planted for us to harvest. Observing our parents, we have the "cheat sheet" to what our struggles and challenges will be in this lifetime. Because we conclude their shortcomings as theirs, they become as disassociated from our reality as the blur of scenery while we travel up a highway at seventy miles an hour. Their character struggles may look different on the surface, because our outer world is generations apart. The specific opposition faced by our parents may be different from ours, but the theme is similar.

In March 2006 my sisters and I were informed that my father had a massive heart attack and was about to undergo open heart surgery, but probably wouldn't survive. An immediate visit to the hospital is not an unusual response for a man's daughters, except we had not spoken to or seen my father in close to thirty years. Still, my sisters and I dropped everything to be at his bedside in Florida. We all wanted to find closure with the man who gave us life. We couldn't consciously articulate why, but for me, the reason unfolded during the trip.

My sisters left the day before I was able to get away. When I called to check in on his condition, they said he had been in and out of consciousness that whole day, but they had the opportunity to speak with him. They said he seemed pleased they were there and understood I was coming as well. By the time I got there, though, he was unconscious. Not knowing if I would ever see him alive, I chose to search for a place of peace around the incompleteness of our relationship.

We spent long stretches of time in the waiting room between the brief visits we were permitted at our father's bedside. Passing the long hours, I sorted through an array of emotions I carried with me about my father. Opposite of counting sheep to fall asleep, I counted all the ways he and I were not alike, before I woke up and saw how alike we were. Connecting the parallels of our lives, I not only came to the realization of who he must be, but also understood myself more. Understanding him allowed me to mend the wounds his absence caused. Simultaneously, I was led to viable insights about my own life.

I had given up a successful real estate practice, retiring from my career early. I was forty-two at the time. Two years later, I discovered that my father was forty-two when he retired from his successful career. I was not involved with my father enough to have known that fact, but when I found out, it got my attention. Years later, I was ready to use that piece of information for my growth. At my father's bedside, I postulated his reason for early retirement must have been similar to mine. He probably couldn't express the disconnectedness he felt from himself or the emptiness that consumed him, irrespective of the successful business he built and the wealth he amassed. Did he, too, attempt to soothe the intensity of an inner ache he didn't understand?

What separated us was how we each waged war with our inner Armageddon. For me, retirement was the pivotal point when I changed my birth destiny. If he and I were walking down a similar path, it was at retirement that I made a sharp turn, whereas he continued to travel the same familiar, yet barren, road. The validation was in his life. He drank daily; he remained in the same unharmonious marriage with his second wife; and he was always fighting a battle of some injustice that had been done to him. As his progeny, what I witnessed on my visit was a mirror reflection of a life I could have chosen, had I continued to make the same decisions he did. Instead, I chose to look inward and therefore took responsibility for my life, which is why it evolved differently from his.

My father's father died from a heart ailment. My father's heart problems showed genetics were at play. Health issues are a symptom of an underlining inner distortion. With that perspective, it makes sense that if we entered the environment at birth appropriate to where we left off, we will naturally magnetize the same health issues our parents have, if we don't change the underlying distortion. Scientifically it is referred to as a genetic predisposition. Although science might argue otherwise, because it would be difficult to quantitatively experiment with it, you can change that gene predisposition by changing your patterns. DNA is a reflection of consciousness and not the cause of consciousness. Accepting this truth is where the ultimate responsibility plays out. The flip side is that family history is not a death sentence. As consciousness changes, our DNA reflects that change.

"In the last decade, epigenetic research has established that DNA blueprints passed down through genes are not set in concrete at birth. Genes are not destiny! Environmental influences, including nutrition, stress, and emotions, can modify those genes, without changing their basic blueprint. And those modifications, epigeneticists have discovered, can be passed on to future generations as surely as DNA blueprints are passed on via the Double Helix." (Reik and Walter 2001; Surani 2001) *The Biology of Belief* by Bruce Lipton, Ph.D.

Life is a moving force that flows through us. When we direct that energy with unawareness, we funnel that energy into the patterns of history. When we connect to our inner knowing, we follow the flow of our Spirit. The pivotal points give us the opportunity to use our energy to recreate a future different from our past and from the past of the lineage we follow.

"When we cross that line and truly understand the New Biology, we will no longer fractiously debate the role of nurture and nature, because we will realize that the fully conscious mind trumps both nature and nurture." *The Biology of Belief* by Bruce Lipton, Ph.D.

THE PATTERN

There is no coming to consciousness without pain.

—Carl Jung

When we are immersed in the life experience, it often takes more than several similar experiences to recognize we are stuck in a continuous loop, reenacting a pattern. A familiar theme that consistently shows up in our reality indicates a pattern. It's not the repetitive pattern that typically gets our attention, but the pain that tails the pattern that makes us take a closer look. Without the emotional pain that follows, we would continue to replicate our experiences with little notice of how they usurp our energy, cutting our potential short. Contrary to popular belief, emotional pain is not our foe. It is actually a friend, but not a fair-weather friend. Pain is always present when we need it. Similar to the reliable beacon on a lighthouse flashing to help ships find their way through the thickest fog, sometimes pain is the only signal we notice through the fog of our distorted beliefs. It is a signal attempting to guide us in a different direction, but often we paint over the pain with the busyness of living, almost to the point that the pain is not recognizable. When nothing about our life changes, we continue reenacting a pattern. Instead of living, we endure. Like the hamster on a wheel, no matter how fast or furious, our movement doesn't take us anywhere new.

Our emotional reactions are a symptom of pain. If we look closer, the reaction can lead us to the underlying issue we defend, the one keeping us from change. What we defend is a distorted belief supporting the pattern running our life, and all along we thought we were the ones in control.

For example, Candice was a brilliant, beautiful, and high-spirited woman who displayed a tremendous amount of strength and courage, yet her life was a swirl of chaos. She bounced from one emotional episode to the next, leaving little time for her to manage her life comfortably. The pattern she enacted over and over again was her inability to say no. She was constantly pulled in different directions by others begging favors. Whether she liked or disliked the person didn't matter. She willingly, even though sometimes begrudgingly, enabled those who asked for help. She came to their aid, sometimes at the cost of her values, because often the people she helped were opposed to her convictions about right and wrong. She expressed her feelings when she was pushed into exhaustion. In those moments, she lashed out in anger beyond the appropriate level of response to what occurred, and rarely was her anger directed where it belonged. Her inability to say no kept her life in a simmer, building up pressure until she couldn't take anymore. The chaos in which she lived masked the pain she was afraid to touch. The pattern had a utilitarian use, avoiding pain, but the byproduct of its function was similar to the factory smoke stacks that billow out white clouds of pollutants; just like the factory, the pattern served a purpose, but the cost was toxic.

Candice believed if she let herself feel, she would not be in control of her life, and she wouldn't be able to function, because the pain would be unbearable. What she couldn't see was her painful feelings were the catalyst to transmute a different action. Instead she was imprisoned by the pattern. Any time the pattern played out in her life, she buckled under the dominion of the pattern rather than becoming the ruler of her own life. Where she appeared generous, her giving wasn't about generosity. It was an outer motion used as a distraction, rather than an expression of inner creativity developed over a lifetime of experiences. She could not give of herself because she had no relationship with herself; she was too busy running away from her pain.

The patterns in our life are similar to stencils on photography lights. The stenciled shapes, meant to meet the need of the lighting, are rarely noticeable to the untrained eye, because they blend into the background. We look at our life with an untrained eye when we believe what is occurring is happening to us, rather than its being brought about as the result of a stencil we designed to meet the need of our distorted beliefs. If we believe, like Candice, that pain is too difficult to work through, we will create a pattern to avoid feeling it. The irony is the pattern will grow more painful over time. If we train ourselves to find the patterns in our life, we can chip away at the repetition of a negative theme by responding differently. Chipping away at patterns sounds minimal on purpose. At the conscious level, it will take eons to remove an unconscious pattern.

Are We Doomed?

Because my psychic friend knew we influence our future by what we do in the present, he felt predicting a future was too limiting, so he preferred to educate his clients on how they can eliminate the suffering he could foretell. For instance, during a reading, if he saw illness in a client's future, he determined what distorted belief structure the client was abiding by that would eventually reflect the distortion in her physical health. He brought to her attention the implicit, but pervasive, pattern that was causing her energy to constrict. He endeavored to help his clients become free from the hardship of self-imposed limits. Clients left the session exuberant and full of optimism, yet to his dismay, the priceless information he conveyed rarely changed a thing. Clients rarely prevented the future difficulties he ascertained for them, but tried to prevent. Clients came back months later in the same pain, wanting answers about the same issue or a more intensely painful issue that had developed.

It goes something like this: Sally B. was depressed because once again she was in an unsatisfactory relationship. Not only was she financially supporting both herself and Bob, but she also took on the responsibility for his emotional needs. No matter how hard she tried, she couldn't encourage any positive change in his mood. She blamed herself, and he blamed her for all that was not right between them, as well as in his life. She tried everything to make it different. Without hesitation, she took over all of Bob's debt when he got laid off. He promised her it would be temporarily, but eight months passed. His job hunt, which started out enthusiastically, fizzled out to his looking at the Want Ads once a week. Sally wondered if he believed that by reading them and doing nothing more, as if by osmosis he would be hired for a job. He got his son every other weekend and preferred to watch sports on television than interact with the ten-year-old. Sally usually felt sorry for the boy and ended up taking him shopping, where she bought some toy he wanted, but certainly didn't need. It went on and on and over and over. Sally continued to exonerate Bob from participating in their relationship as an equal, while simultaneously taking on more responsibility for his life.

My psychic friend told her, "Unless you break your relationship pattern, beginning by being responsible for yourself and not Bob, your health will deteriorate." They discussed it in depth and even uncovered the issues underpinning her lack of self-worth, which kept her co-dependant on such a thoughtless partner.

Together she and the psychic invalidated the fears that prevented her from taking care of herself. They discussed what she needed to do and how she could prepare for the difficult adjustment that change causes. She said to my friend, "Yes, I believe my health is already suffering. I want to leave him."

Every few months, Sally B. returned for a psychic reading, and she and my friend repeated the interaction. As if on cue, Sally repeated, "Yes, I believe my health is already suffering. I want to leave him."

My friend hadn't seen Sally B. in more than a year. The next time she came for a psychic reading, she was still with Bob, but the relationship was no longer her primary concern. She told my friend she was battling thyroid cancer and wanted to know her odds of surviving.

"The light at the end of the tunnel is an oncoming train!" No matter how many times he tells his clients the direction they are heading in is the path of a train, they continue in the same direction, as if memorized by a glimmer of light at the end of the dark tunnel. Part of the delusion is that the scenery will change while heading down the same path. As it appears succinctly in the *Basic Text of Narcotics Anonymous*, "Insanity is repeating the same mistakes and expecting different results."

After a twenty-plus-year friendship with my psychic friend, I can testify most of his life has been spent guiding his clients away from the path of the oncoming train and then being there to help pick up the pieces after the crash, because they didn't do anything different. It didn't take long into his thirty-five years of giving psychic readings before he resigned himself to his role as a shoulder his client's cried on while they went through life's trials and tribulations. He has moved past the frustration of a parent schooling his child not to play with matches and then being there to help soothe the burns after the child burns her finger.

A self-help group I participated in took eradicating unfavorable patterns to another level. The lead instructor dissected a student's life to identify the most adverse pattern and did gestalt work to eliminate it. The instructor linked the pattern back to the student's childhood and had the student reenact the past to change the future. For instance, if someone attracted the same negative dynamic in a relationship over and over, the instructor linked that pattern back to a negative experience with a parent as the root cause. Next the student picked someone in the classroom who resembled the parent and talked to that person, but in the imagined timeline of the past. The purpose was to release the feelings a child could not verbalize, but felt. The intent was to loosen pent-up emotions that suppressed the adult expression, the ones responsible for the repetitive patterns.

The friend who recommended the weekend class attended it herself and couldn't stop talking about it. She encouraged me to sign up. My initial response was something like, "There is no way I could sit through a weekend self-help course, when I have trouble sitting through a day-long seminar past the lunch break."

"No," she said, "this is different. You won't want it to end."

She was right. The course was more entertainment than any Oscar-winning movie. The emotional intensity, tension, and drama kept me spellbound all weekend. The premise was self-actualization through self-disclosure, and the weekend was filled with activities to facilitate both. Since the most horrid stories told about a student's childhood were reciprocated with attention, the environment motivated the students to reveal any and all life trauma. Students who didn't normally like being in the spotlight eventually gave in, hypnotized by the emotional swirl that overtook the weekend. Self-disclosure innocently transformed into self-presentation, where the truth may have been ever-so-slightly manipulated to glean more sympathy. Boxes of Kleenex were scattered throughout the room, and though they seemed odd at the onset, they were a high-demand commodity as the weekend progressed.

I regretted each time I had to use the bathroom, because I didn't want to miss something remarkable. Some attendees claimed the weekend experience was as memorable as the birth of their child. While it may run parallel to the emotional intensity of childbirth, less than remarkable were the results. I never witnessed a lasting change in any student after the course, not even in myself. If there was any positive change, it was brief, and the damaging pattern the instructor tried to disseminate came back with a vengeance, as if the momentary reprieve gave it the rest it needed to gain more momentum.

Once we completed the weekend class, we were permitted to attend any future classes as angels. The angels were helpers. As I continued to attend as an angel, I noticed each class had its star student who appeared to make the biggest leap forward in self-awareness. During one class the hero was a student whose self-awareness soared when she finally admitted that she submitted to her husband's brutality. For the first time in her life she vocalized that she had become like her mother, whom she detested. The emotional and physical abuse she tolerated in her marriage was no different from the abuse she watched, with disgust, her mother accept from her father. Like her mother, any interests she had became secondary to her husband's demands. She sacrificed her life while being submissive to her husband.

In class she picked another student who represented her father. She screamed at him with all the anger she could muster, much more than she expected. She then spoke to a second student, whom she picked to stand in as her husband. She brought the house down when she told the surrogate husband she wanted a divorce. All the applause and cheering made the spectators of any sporting event sound meek by comparison. When I couldn't fathom any more enthusiasm, she added that she was going back to school to fulfill her dreams. She pronounced to the husband stand-in that she expected him to support her financially during that period, since she sacrificed ten years of her life fulfilling his needs. A second round of excitement echoed the room. The final exercise to imprint the newfound hope in her psyche was a skit where she acted out her new envisioned life filled with career success and a new love. The class lifted her off the ground as everyone cheered her on and celebrated her with a dance and group hug. Filled with the energy from the class, she left with a sense of power, ready to conquer her problems. All the encouragement over the weekend lit the flame of passion within her. She was motivated to go out and create a new life.

If you jump start a damaged car battery, not only will the charge not hold, but it can also cause more problems to the car. Along the same lines, she is still in the same marriage, years later, and her dream of going back to school never materialized. No longer does she vocalize the cost to stay. Instead she has stacked layers of justification to back the reason she stayed and the reason she never went back to school. She offers her excuses whether or not asked. It's as if she used her boost of energy at the end of the course to strengthen her resistance to change. Any flicker of hope was smothered, and the once-vibrant woman has become numb to the wrongness in her life.

Change is not easy; most of us can more easily justify why we don't change, rather than doing the work necessary to bring about change. The patterns that appear in all aspects of our life are more vivid in love relationships. When a love relationship has gone bad, it is easier to identify the source of the consequential pain. Amplified by the contrast to what was once so good, the extreme prods us to take a closer look at what happened. As the choreographer of our relationships, we became enthralled by the familiar steps of our relationship dance, even when the dance is emotionally exhausting. It is a beautiful dance, in that each participant in the relationship masterfully plays out his or her part with graceful ease. When the final act concludes, we can look back and see the perfect dance was not unique to the relationship, but was a dance we follow to the music of love.

No matter how different the new person I entered into a relationship with seemed to be from the person before, the dance remained the same. Each relationship followed a distinct pattern, and before the relationship ended, to my surprise, the person I was involved with had an uncanny resemblance to the person before. I didn't understand. None of them started out being the same. How did they all end up being the same?

My fear of being alone formed the hub of the wheel around which my relationships revolved. It's ironic, because ever since I could walk and talk, I was independent. I never did what my mother told me, so out of frustration, she would say, "Sofia, you don't need a mother."

Whenever I heard her say it, I would think, "You are right, so stop telling me what to do." I grew up to be an independent woman who never depended on anyone for anything, yet this independent woman was afraid to be alone. To compensate, when one relationship ended, my mission was to find the next.

Our unconscious is the great enabler of our fears. We can see someone across a room, and before we've had an opportunity to have a conversation with that person, our unconscious knows that person's capabilities. My unconscious, if it had a voice, was therefore saying, "Hey, Sofia, if you are afraid to be alone, don't worry. I will find you the neediest people out there to partner with, and you will never be left." By anyone's initial observation, these potential suitors appeared self-reliant, but after they sucked the life out of me, I did everything to disengage from the relationship—everything except break up, since I was afraid to be alone. The person I was with would eventually end the relationship, and I would be left feeling stupid, trying to piece together what happened, wondering, "Maybe I shouldn't have worked so much; maybe we should have taken more vacations."

I went into therapy to understand the pattern that prevailed in my relationships. While I felt privileged to have worked with several talented and insightful psychologists, what I was told, over and over, was that my fear of being alone was a response to abandonment. What a strong diagnosis given to the mere fact my parents divorced when I was two! I was happy my father was not a large part of my life, because he and I never got along, but because I was told over and over that their divorce was a big loss in my life, I began to identify with the loss. While it gave me a reason for what otherwise didn't make sense, it still did not change my need to enter into relationships to avoid being alone and to stay in them for the same reason, long after it was evident they were not compatible relationships. Even though I enjoyed the candor of the conversations with my psychologists, all the analyzing didn't lessen my irrational fear or change the pattern in my subsequent relationships.

"I was abandoned" felt like a badge of courage equivalent to re-ceiving a purple heart for bravery, but it did nothing to change my reality. Not satisfied with my progress in therapy, I continued my quest to figure out how to conquer my illogical fear so I could break my negative relationship pattern. My next place of exploration was a past-life regressionist. Since my current life conclusions did nothing to diminish my fear, it seemed logical to presume it was something from a past life.

The past-life regressionist said, "You led troops into war. Your troops were killed, so you were alone. It was a horrid loneliness, because you were wrought with guilt and sadness from losing your troops."

While I was being told this tale, and I emphasize the word *tale*, all I kept thinking was, "What a terrible leader I must have been if I survived while everyone I was in charge of died." Needless to say, I left feeling even less comforted and further from resolution.

When all else failed, I tried sheer will influenced by *A Beautiful Mind*. The film portrayed a true story about a brilliant, Nobel-prize-winning mathematician who was schizophrenic. Not able to tolerate the medication that dulled the voices in his mind because it also dulled his brilliance, he became determined not to take the medicine. Resorting to the use of a strong will, he stopped focusing on the voices in his mind. Daily he battled his illness through determination and will. His heroic effort inspired me. If he could do what he did, certainly I could end my relationship pattern. I started by ending the incompatible relationship I was in at the time.

Giving kudos to the movie that inspired my strength, I knew my next relationship would be different, now that I broke my pattern and ended my current relationship, regardless of my fear of being alone. I knew my next love would be really good for me and would be someone I could share my life with. It worked for a year and a half, until the same old pattern reared its ugly head. I was confused. What was I missing?

I thought I had chosen distinctly different people, but in hindsight, the differences justified the relationship. The greater the effort I put forth to understand what happened, the more impotent I felt to change the inevitable outcome. I believed a relationship was not meant to be, as though what happened to me was like what happens to an innocent bystander getting shot by the bullets meant for someone else.

Since the poisonous pattern does not originate at the physical level where it manifests, neither does the antidote. If it were that simple, as my psychic friend found out, as the class I took demonstrated, and as the result of my effort in therapy evidenced, once we identified a pattern, we could successfully change it. While sometimes it seems we have changed a pattern, unwittingly we have replaced it. The replacement registers in our conscious mind as insignificantly as changing an order in a restaurant. "Oh, you don't have Coke? Pepsi will do." We don't even notice. What seems like a new theme only supplants the old.

Our reflex of replacing one behavior with another of like kind is actually an innate safety device our unconscious calls forth to prevent an internal avalanche. Similarly, the proper construction of a home foresees the potential for structural weakness and incorporates safeguards. During a construction project I managed, the completion of the cedar front porch would have been delayed while we awaited the delivery of the cedar beams. Rather than bringing the project to a halt, the subcontractors doing the work continued to build the portico, but temporarily supported it with plain wooden beams. Once the cedar beams arrived, the wood beams were replaced. Had the carpenters taken out the supports before the cedar beams went in, the roof that graced the doorway would have collapsed. Likewise, if we remove the beliefs our patterns revolve around before a new concept is adopted, instability will jeopardize our ability to function, as witnessed with emotional breakdowns.

The Mustard Seed

The patterns we reflect physically begin at the level before physical manifestation, at the level of the unconscious. Our debilitating patterns are the life-force of our Spirit, taking the form of repetitive patterns dictated by our unconscious, distorted beliefs, rather than refracting the pure intent of our Spirit, which is to grow. We cannot eliminate a behavior structure that supports an unconscious belief by consciously replacing the belief. Just as a virus in our computer can project onto the monitor a picture different from what we consciously command, our unconscious is the operating system that projects on our reality a picture different from our conscious intent.

The conundrum is that manifestation is molded from three directives of consciousness that are often out of sync: the conscious level, the unconscious level, and the soul level. Just as a woman can be a mother, a sister, and a daughter, consciousness is one, but means something different, depending on the level dominating the moment. If only the levels of consciousness we operate under were under the jurisdiction of soul-level consciousness! As we observe our life, the areas where we emotionally react are an indication we are not under the jurisdiction of our soul, as it transforms the intent of our Spirit.

The biblical mustard seed that has the strength to move the mountain of our repetitive patterns is the power of our Spirit as directed by soul-level consciousness. When the levels of consciousness are out of sync, the force of life is diminished as it flows through us seeking balance rather than moving us with our potential.

A high school girl went into confession where she said, "Father, I have sinned. Twice this week I lied to my mother; I cursed four times; and I had sex."

The priest's reply unnerved the girl; all he said was "Okay."

"But Father, she pleaded, don't you want me to pray for my sins?"

"No, you can pray all you want, but all you are doing is projecting your unbalanced essence into the world. The world would be better off if you asked yourself these three questions. Why did I lie to my mother? Why did I curse? Why did I have sex?"

Sill stunned, she cried out, "Father, does it matter to God why I sinned? Please just give me my due punishment."

"My dear child, the biggest blasphemy is not knowing thyself. God doesn't care what you do until then, because you are useless to God if you are not expressing yourself."

THE MAGIC BOTTLE

O nce upon a time there was a popular interior designer, Jean Louis. He had an eye for beauty, and because of it found some of the most distinguished accent pieces for his clients in places most people would abhor being caught inside. On top of his list of frequent stops were obscure flea markets filled with other people's discarded junk and cluttered estate sales hosted by family members eager to be rid of the material remains of relatives who passed away. Since Jean Louis's mother sold antiques, he was raised to find the golden needle in the haystack of stuff. His heart filled with joy when he found a valuable item unrecognized by the seller, and Jean Louis gleefully accepted the role of negotiator. Watching him was like watching the graceful movements of an illusionist. You had to look for the deliberate steps he took; otherwise you would miss his crafty manipulation, which led the sellers to believe they took advantage of him. It was not unusual for the seller to be in tow as he walked to his car, thanking him profusely— a culmination of guilt and relief. The fact that the seller had nothing to feel bad about was the secret Jean Louis carried all the way to the bank.

One rainy Friday afternoon, Jean Louis's life took a different direction. The day started off similar to most days in the life of Jean Louis's, consumed with work. The task at hand was searching for an ornate chest to accent the décor of a room he designed for the Atlanta Tour of Homes. Since there was not enough time to refinish a hidden gem he could steal from an unwitting, unsophisticated seller, he went where he was guaranteed to find what he needed. He made his way to an area of town that hosted many upscale antique shops that ran side by side for blocks. He walked in and out of each store until he found what he was looking for, an ornate chest. On top of the chest sat a dingy bottle. Surrounded by well-preserved, clean, beautiful collections from the past, the bottle appeared out of place and surely not a complement to the ornate chest it rested on. When he went to move the bottle from the chest he was ready to buy, the price tag caught his attention. Though he was not the least bit interested in the bottle, he was curious about its history, since the price insinuated an interesting past. He asked the clerk, "Why is this bottle so expensive? Did it belong to someone famous?"

The clerk responded, "The bottle belonged to a young king who lost his kingdom, but that is not why it is so pricey. What makes it so valuable is what is inside. The bottle contains energy. All you need to do is give the energy an order, and it will perform whatever task you wish of it."

A magic bottle! Jean Louis was delighted. He had said to his beloved the day before that he wished there were two of him. Now he had a solution to his daily grind of too much to do in too little time. Without further regard to its price or history, he said, "I'll buy it!"

The clerk was quick to respond, "I must warn you. Never let the energy out of the bottle if you are uncertain about what you want it to accomplish. You must always direct it carefully. If you remember nothing more, whatever you do, never leave the lid off, if you have not given it precise orders."

Jean Louis was already lost in his head with all the ideas he had for the bottle and how the extra energy could help him create the life of his dreams. He felt as if he had won the lottery. What the clerk was talking on about was no longer his concern. The only regard he had for what she said was she was a fool to think for a second he'd waste any of the precious energy inside the bottle. He knew he would always find something constructive for it to do. A normally solemn man, he left the store with the bottle in hand and his lips curled in a smile he could not contain.

True to the shop clerk's word, without fail or complaint, the extra energy did everything he asked of it in the six months that he owned the bottle. As a result, each succeeding month, his income nearly doubled from the prior month. Jean Louis found his mood light and cheerful for the first time in a long time. He was thrilled by how much he could get done with the aid of the extra energy in the bottle. It followed the list he methodically prepared for it daily.

Jean Louis was realizing his dreams of financial success as well as the time to enjoy his accumulating wealth. That's not all. On top of his skyrocketing income, he became regarded as one of the most sought-after designers. The recognition was not limited to his native state of Georgia, either. The calls he received included the personal assistants of some of the most prominent entertainment icons in Hollywood. He went to bed each night thinking, "If I don't wake up in the morning, I will have died a happy man."

He had an interview scheduled in Los Angeles to design a second home for an up-and-coming Hollywood actress. Since it had been well over two years since Jean Louis had taken time off, the tail end of the business trip would be a perfect way to accommodate a vacation with his beloved, who had waited patiently. Now that he was able to accomplish so much more with the aid of the energy in the bottle, Jean Louis could finally make good on his promise that they would get away as soon as he found the time.

He decided the bottle needed a break, too, because the minute he returned, his workload would be overwhelming. On top of an already full schedule, he would be traveling to LA. In his rush to leave, though, he forgot to put the lid on the bottle. He remembered while he was lying on a beach thousands of miles away sipping on a sugary beach drink. The thought left his mind as fast as it came. He didn't think too much about it, because the bottle always cooperated. In Jean Louis's mind there was no reason to worry. He thought the shop clerk, like most women, overreacted with her nearly hysteric warning.

When he returned, all tanned and refreshed, he hailed a cab to take him home from the airport, but when he got to his street, his house was gone. Only ashes and remnants of charred lumber remained. What happened? When he got out of the cab, he searched around dumbfounded, and then he saw it—the bottle. It was on the ground fully intact, with its lid several inches away. His mind flashed back to when he was lying on the beach, unconcerned about the open bottle of energy, because he trusted it. Furious, he picked it up and smashed it to the ground. Next he went straight to the shop where he bought it. He threw the door open with such force that everyone inside looked his way. As soon as he made eye contact with the clerk who sold him the bottle, he screamed at her, "Your bottle has ruined me! While I was on vacation, the energy in the bottle set my home on fire."

The shopkeeper looked at him with disgust. "You fool, I warned you. Don't you know energy creates as well as it destroys? I told you never to leave it unattended."

Haven't we all had similar moments when we look at life in disbelief and wonder, "Why is this happening to me?" Unraveling the mystery starts with what gets our attention, and more often than not, it is the loss of something meaningful. Tracing the steps backwards, we try to figure out why it happened, but our clarity is clouded by fear. The fear is that at any moment life as we know it can be pulled out from under us. We can lose our job, our status, a relationship, a loved one, our health, etc. We believe if we find something to blame for what appears as a sudden destruction of form, we will feel better. What felt like a tsunami is more like waves of energy slowly threatening what appears a solid reality. Even more daunting, we chose to believe we have nothing to do with how energy creates and destroys our reality, when in fact we orchestrate its ebb and flow, which means we have the capacity to change our reality with every moment.

A passage attributed to Nelson Mandela has a line that says it well, "Our deepest fear is not that we are inadequate. Our deepest fear is that we are powerful beyond measure…"

A Fourteen-Letter Word

The first law of thermodynamics states, "Energy can neither be created nor destroyed." If energy is channeled into the creation of a form—manifestation—it is the form that can be created and destroyed, not the force of energy.

How the infinite power of energy is molded into creation has always been left up to God. Although we gave him the responsibility for our life, we felt the need to guide his hand with prayer, and naturally, God carried the burden of our disappointment when life didn't go as we hoped.

The advent of quantum physics took God off the hot seat. It portrays creation in a way that reconciles what wise teachers such as Jesus, Plato, Aristotle, Socrates, Pythagoras, Lao Tzu, Confucius, and Buddha implied thousands of years ago. Quantum physics verifies that the force of life, as the material that forms our physical world, is not molded into form by an external god.

According to the Gospel of Thomas, more than two thousand years ago, Jesus said, "If your leaders say to you, 'Look, the kingdom is in heaven,' then the birds of heaven will precede you. If they say to you, 'It is in the sea,' then the fish will precede you. Rather, the kingdom is inside you and it is outside you." In other words, God is the life-force that permeates everything in existence. We direct the force of God that is within us. It is the energy we use to manifest in the physical world, and equally as powerfully the cause of the destruction of what we have created, although the destruction is often felt as disappointing.

Discoveries in quantum physics implicate how we mold life-force. The observer is the impetus that influences how subatomic matter takes form. What we, the observer, expect is what we mold into reality. Experiments that quantified the theory discovered that if scientist Smith expected to see particles under the microscope, he would, whereas if scientist Wilson expected to see waves under the microscope, he would.

We channel the force of energy and transmute it into a form compatible with who we are. If we mold energy into manifestation through the expectation of our purpose, any concept we hold that is not compatible with our potential will stand fixed in opposition as energy continues to collide against it. What is not fit for soul growth will eventually be shattered through our experiences. The physical world speaks a language that translates our internal world, which is why we need to understand what our experiences communicate. If we continue to hold on to what is no longer appropriate with the flow of our life, resistance to that flow will ramp up the intensity of those experiences until we reach the point of realization from a difficult lesson learned. It is through the destruction of one form that energy is released to create what is more compatible for our purpose.

When I was involved with a spiritual community, I reached a point where my ability to continue learning was blocked by my concerns over the dysfunctional dynamics among the people. It was difficult for me to work through the inner conflict, because my influence had no impact. It reminded me of my family enmeshment when I grew up, where the individual roles were set in place and any movement threatened the whole. I felt no resolve was possible if I stayed.

Oddly, leaving wasn't a simple solution. On one hand I felt distain for the politics that formed the structure of the community, but on the other hand, I felt comforted by the familiarity of the people. Whichever side of the internal conflict I chose, the opposing side pulled me back. I was in a rut. Depending on the day or the perceived indiscretion, I either made allowances for the politics that made the environment feel constrained or I went on a rampage about the injustice. When I was protecting my pattern of not wanting to be alone, I ignored any incidents that got my attention. What couldn't be ignored I justified. On other days, I focused on what I perceived as wrong, similar to how a teenager gossips with one friend about another friend behind her back. I was oblivious to the inner tension building, because my need to belong overshadowed the ping pong match in my head. Since the ball was returned as fast as it landed, there was no time for self-reflection. The chaos of conflict stirred up a lot of mental activity that prevented any truth. It was activity without movement, because I remained in an environment meant to facilitate self-awareness while denying what was true for me.

When the events of a day viewed through the binoculars of hindsight point to a cause responsible for changing destiny, we believe one event changed our fate. We focus so much on the manifested reality that we overlook the inner tension shifting the underpinnings of our reality. What appears to be one life changing event has been occurring over time. The outcome is providence. I define providence as the pivotal point that has the potential to get us back on our path if we surrender to it. My day of providence started with my offer to purchase a plot of land to develop four home sites.

Since I had bought, sold, and developed real estate for years, nothing was abnormal about the offer. Consciously, I had no indication I lit a stick of dynamite. It didn't take long after it was ignited for my crystallized comfort to shatter. The lead instructor of the spiritual community lived in the area, and I was accused of being disrespectful because the property was close to her home. The uproar and accusations against me were too harsh to brush off and too hurtful to retaliate. I was left no choice but to leave.

I found it difficult to agree with a belief that concludes I willingly mold my reality, especially when it credits me for the difficulties in my life. Certainly, I wouldn't choose to create those experiences, so the question that begs an answer is this: what part of me is the observer molding my reality?

Over and over again it has been proven to me that if something occurs in my reality, the question is not whether I had a part in it, but what part of me had a part in it. In the above example, I suspect it was the part that always knows what is right for my growth, but since it was in conflict with the part that was afraid of being alone, the collision of the two was responsible for the eruption necessary for me to break free. The part of me that knows what is best is not concerned about how I am redirected, just as a parent isn't concerned about his child's comfort while he is whisking her out of a party long past her curfew. Nothing happens without divine authority—the divinity within me.

The Division of Consciousness

Although consciousness is synonymous with soul, in the laboratory of life we can dissect consciousness into three levels. We therefore each have three observers—the conscious mind, the unconscious mind, and the superconscious mind. Similarly, our home may have different levels and rooms, although each is under the auspices of the home. How I occupy my home is a perfect model to delineate the three levels of consciousness.

My basement is mostly unfinished. There is one finished room in my basement that I use as a film-editing studio. My studio is a place that I discipline myself to go, and the work I do there requires focus. The space it takes up is a fraction of the total home. It coincides with my conscious mind by my deliberation to go there, the focus required to get anything done there, and the ratio of space it consumes in comparison to the total.

The main level of my house contains the rooms where I spend the most time. My kitchen, family room, and office are located on the main level. Sometimes I wander around on the main level aimlessly. Often it is without a purpose other than what strikes my attention in the moment. I am not even aware that I have opened the refrigerator for the third time, as though I were expecting to find something different from what I saw the two times before. Often I go through all the cable channels over and over, maybe several times, before it dawns on me that nothing worth watching is on. In my office I begin one task and switch to a more interesting task before the first one is complete, circling back around to the first, but often not in the same day. Not only is the size of the space and the time I spend on the main level of my home proportionate to the size and the time I spend without conscious thought, but also the lack of forethought about how I wander around there is similar.

The upstairs of my home is where I sleep. I go there at least once a day, but don't spend much awake time upstairs. Once I am asleep, it is usually the most peaceful time of each day, similar to how our lives would be if we allowed the soul level of consciousness to direct our lives, with the other levels of consciousness under its domain.

In the upstairs level, I have a hidden closet where I can keep valuable things. The closet of valuables can symbolize my Spirit, as its intent is reachable through the soul level.

No wonder life often looks different from our plans. We rely on a conscious mind equal to about ten percent of consciousness when the other ninety percent we are oblivious to has far more impact on our lives. We are unsuspecting of the other observers we house in consciousness. The part of consciousness that dominates the role of the observer is usually unconscious to our conscious mind. While our conscious mind is tenuous, like the teenager who folds under pressure, the unconscious mind is the strength that dominates the reign of authority over our life, and more often than not, it is responsible for how energy is molded into our reality. The irrationality of reality has thus been made rational.

When Carol and Barb toasted New Year's Eve, they had no idea they were about to embark of the quagmire of consciousness. That was the furthest thing from their mind, since they were dedicating the year to losing weight. Carol and Barb made a New Year's resolution to lose one hundred pounds between them and agreed to attend a seminar on the latest fad diet that claimed unprecedented results.

Before January was over, full of excitement and anticipation, they drove to the seminar together. They spent most of their thirty-minute drive discussing how much better their lives would be without the excess weight. Their conversation clothed them in the latest fashions, had the most eligible bachelors propose to them, and offered them new, exciting careers. They headed to the seminar with high hopes. Neither left disappointed or empty-handed. They each purchased the book that outlined the premise of the program and the self-help affirmation CD, which was essential to listen to and repeat before each meal. They ordered a month's supply of the delicious low-calorie food they sampled. They headed into week two at close to a fifty-fifty split of the fifteen pounds they lost between them. Three weeks later they began bootcamp at a local gym. Their family and friends called them the dynamic duo. Their dedication and determination was an inspiration to those who cheered them on.

Two months later, their weight changed significantly. Between Barb and Carol, the scales tipped twenty-seven pounds more, with neither one weighing less than when they began.

The conscious application of what we think and what we feel may fasten together pieces of life to make our decisions seem logical, but what we determine as logical is clouded by the strength and sway of our unconscious mind. Our unconscious mind uses the conscious mind to aid and abet the execution of its underlying motives. In a split-second decision, our unconscious mind can oppose the logic of our conscious mind, and then we quickly use our conscious mind to rally logic around the decision to make us comfortable.

When I spoke with Barb and Carol, my first question was, "How did it happen? You both seemed so determined to lose weight and get into shape. You even had each other for motivation and support."

Carol answered with smile, "The first time we fell off the wagon, a cold front had hit, announcing winter was officially here. I distinctly remember it was a Wednesday, the second night of bootcamp for that week. I called Barb to say 'Let's skip bootcamp tonight. We have been so good up until now, one night won't make us fatter.' That same night, I went to the grocery store and bought all my favorite snacks. Hell, if I was going to blow off bootcamp, I might as well have fun. I looked at it as I would a night out drinking with my friends, where I push the limits of my usual behavior because of the infrequency of the activity. Except in this case my friends were the different varieties sugar comes in."

Barb laughed as she chimed in. "I was bad that night too. I called another friend and we went to my favorite restaurant full of southern fried cooking. I felt it was meant to be, because I caught Elaine right before she was heading home from work. Elaine was thrilled by my offer. She had a rough day and was in the mood to indulge."

Justification not tempered by the knowing of soul-level consciousness rapes and pillages truth by distorting it to fit the mold of our unconscious expectations. Because our unconscious is a force to our conscious mind, it is a higher frequency, which is why it has a greater influence over our reality than our conscious mind. The conscious mind is not the solid form we are accustomed to in the physical world but demarks the densest form on the hierarchy of consciousness. It is the liaison between consciousness and the material world, but has the least impact on how we manifest in the world. The unconscious mind initiates energy at the level of particles and waves, often bringing forth into manifestation, to our dismay, a different reality than the one we planned. Since the unconscious mind is at a higher frequency and thus stronger than our conscious mind, sometimes the best we can do with our conscious mind is justify the why, because we don't understand how we get in certain predicaments ourselves.

It has been said that this life is but one stop at a train station in the midst of a long journey. Our formidable unconscious mind houses an accumulation of both past-life and present-life memories. If we come into each lifetime with a new conscious mind, but our unconscious mind is a collection of the past, it is easy to conceive its awareness and motives are not limited to the experiences of one lifetime. It's like getting a new computer, but using the old hard drive. As our unconscious mind adheres to a residue of concepts, our emotions are often triggered by an echo of a memory that dominates any conscious reasoning, regardless of whether the magnitude of emotions is out of place in the present. Since the unconscious mind cannot distinguish a past lifetime from last week, some of our greatest fears cannot be legitimized from one lifetime. The illogical process of our unconscious has been a fascination that has been studied for centuries in attempts to make it logical within one lifetime.

Joan, for example, was an intelligent, independent woman who had an irrational fear of fire. No conscious logic could make the fear congruent with any current life experience. When her heat went out in inclement weather, she chose to bundle up in blankets rather than light a fire in the huge fireplace that was the focal point of her home. She had plenty of wood to keep her warm over the twelve-hour period she was without heat. The sellers of her home were proud of the precisely stacked and aged wood they left behind as a gift. Her gourmet kitchen would have delighted many five-star chefs, because it featured an expensive, new, commercial-grade gas stove, but she changed it to electric, immediately after closing on the home. In addition to the cost of a new stove, she went to the effort and expense to retrofit her kitchen to accommodate the electric stove, which was no easy task.

The soul level of consciousness is the least-developed observer of consciousness, because during the process of evolution, while we learned to be adept at maneuvering physically, we grew attached to what felt good. Our attachment kept us stuck in the garden of good and evil, because we remembered.

It sounds like a contradiction to say our unconscious mind gravitates to what feels good, when Carol and Barb both say they would enjoy life more if they lost weight. Their sense of wellbeing would escalate if they felt better physically. Oddly, unconsciously we are comforted by familiar sensations. The fine line between pleasure and pain is stimulation. We seek stimulation in the form we are familiar with, and unfortunately angst, martyrdom, anger, and even emotional pain can be queerly comforting.

We don't move forward with both feet at once. Likewise, each level of consciousness has a role, and when our observers are out of sync, there is a reason. Something needs to be gathered and collected in awareness before we can grow. The physical experience refines consciousness. Energy cycles laterally when we evolve from the propulsion generated by our experiences. Today's lesson becomes a memory in our unconscious tomorrow. An accumulation of unconscious memories weighted differently will cause a shift in our patterns, allowing us to create a reality more compatible with who we are.

Today when I hear "You create your own existence," I have to ask, what part of me is creating it? When I hear "If you want something, just ask the universe," my response is, "My Spirit really doesn't care if I get that parking space up front. If I am asking for something, what part of me is asking?" Books are written that speak to the conscious mind about how to manipulate energy to gain prosperity, a promising love life, and so forth. From the level of my soul, a summons is unnecessary, since I will draw what is appropriate, such as the experiences where life falls into a perfect flow. They are labeled as synchronistic. Synchronicities open us up to new possibilities, creating new pathways in our life. When the unconscious mind dominates the formation of particles and waves, we are in a continuous loop of the past. By reenacting the past we engender entropy, inhibiting any possibilities from an otherwise limitless flow of synchronicities.

There are times when dealing with a customer service department that I find myself locked into a disagreement. Each time I try to make my point, even using different words, my words are irrelevant, because we are stuck in a loop of dissatisfaction, going around and around about the same issue. The only way I know to break the cycle is to take my grievance higher by asking to speak with the supervisor. In life, when we are stuck in a loop of dissatisfaction, it is time to take our grievance to the observer with the highest perspective reachable from a state of balance. We do this by overriding unconscious determination with the conscious application of discipline. It takes discipline to engage in activities where we can reach a state of balance. For me it means taking the time to meditate, ride my bike, weight train, or go for a walk. Those are some of the ways I redistribute energy. Energy was being monopolized by my unconscious mind, but once I take time to do one or several of these activities, I have access from soul-level consciousness. I have some of my most profound realizations in those moments, or shortly thereafter. Similarly, when I awaken in the early morning, my mind points me to the solution of a problem I couldn't resolve while awake the day before. When we access a higher level of thought, concepts are useless, since that level is governed by knowing—not intellectual knowing, but a higher quality of knowing.

When we free up energy so that it is not limited to the desires of our conscious and unconscious observers, we are guided from a heightened perspective. We are not even aware of it. In fact when we desperately search for guidance, we are too attached to something we are afraid to lose, want to get, or want to know, such as the outcome of a decision we need to make. Attachment doesn't allow our energy to cycle higher; it keeps us in an emotional state.

Energy directed by soul consciousness is at a higher frequency. In essence it ignites an inner furnace. Like fire that burns away a solid wall that is otherwise impenetrable, acting from higher awareness burns away what is no longer appropriate for our growth without the painful experience to prove it. A common analogy is the friends who fall away from our inner sphere of influence, and there are no hard feelings or bad experiences to blame. When energy cycles vertically in an uninterrupted flow, the fear and doubt, challengeable both emotionally and intellectually, are replaced by faith and knowing, which have nothing to prove.

Since it is difficult to determine what level of consciousness is creating our world at any given moment, it is not uncommon for us to ask for a sign of validation from our Spirit, the universe, or God, although we ask the question attached to the answer. While we are attached to the answer, energy is used to perpetuate our unconscious expectation, keeping us in a streaming loop of the past, often leaving us confused. "It is a poor sort of memory that only works backwards." *Through the Looking-Glass* by Lewis Carroll.

Though it is difficult to duplicate an experience to quantify it as a scientific experiment, the process I am about to share is the closest I can get without a microscope. In the midst of a recent decision, I became acutely aware how my attachment to the outcome created the outcome. I force-fit synchronistic events rather than allow my reality to be guided by the synchronicities of soul consciousness. In the process, I also became startled by the power I have.

The Feathered Foe

A decision haunted me. Should I get another dog? I turned the decision into an agonizing process. As most learning lessons begin with us innocently justifying our motives, I believed another dog was a solution to expand my dog, Sula's, world. I was convinced she needed a playmate, especially since her world shrank by the constraints I imposed. When her Boston terrier friend was killed in the dog park by a larger dog, I would no longer take Sula to the park. My fenced-in back yard was the next best play haven, but was overtaken by a brave hawk large enough to mistake Sula for prey. Short of killing the hawk, my solution was to find something that would scare him away. He was not threatened by my presence, much less the boat horn I bought. While my ears were ringing from the monster horn I blew in his direction, he cocked his head in a curious movement as though trying to understand the sound.

Once I resigned to the reality that he was as much a part of my yard as the trees, the solution of a built-in playmate for Sula became the answer. The process involved in finding a puppy seemed cut and dried, until it became an obsession. My quest became haunted by the flashbacks of the time and energy Sula required as a puppy. Conflicted about the decision, I decided if it was meant to be, I would be given the signs to move forward or not, hence my first deception: The belief I can leave up to my higher consciousness a decision I am attached to.

Surely finding the perfect breeder was a green light, but then she politely told me she would not sell me a puppy. She mistook my ambivalence as instability. One day I said "yes," and then, after I had a panic attack, I called her back and said, "I am not sure yet." Her dogs were a plane ride away, and though my plan was to coordinate the trip around a visit to a friend in her state, I thought, "Maybe it is just as well, since I find traveling burdensome enough without the extra load of a puppy on my return flight." I noticed my enthusiasm for the trip waned when I was no longer coming home with a little fur ball. I decided if I still felt the longing for the puppy after three days, I would call the breeder and convince her I was actually sane. On that third day, before I called her, I thought, "Gee, it sure would be nice if the puppy was a drive away and not a plane ride away." Almost instantaneously a different breeder I spoke to weeks before called to let me know one of her dogs had puppies. She not only was within a four-hour drive, but also, from the pictures she e-mailed, I fell in love with the puppy she nicknamed Butterfly.

I believed it was a sure sign that the puppy within driving distance was the one I was meant to get. To further emphasize the rightness of it, *Butterfly* means psyche or soul in Greek. "Oh, my God, I am not only Greek, but also the psyche is my primary study." I could not ignore the pieces that were weaving together a quilt of coincidences that all pointed to the puppy nicknamed Butterfly.

I was still hesitant, though. The added responsibility stirred up doubt. The timing was not optimal, because of projects I was trying to complete. Depending on how I felt, I knew who to ask "Should I get another dog?" I knew who would say, "She is adorable, get her," and who would say, "I wouldn't, if I were you." I could have argued for or against either camp, depending on the day. Talking about it at all was like throwing a boulder into emotional waters. My drama created more ripples, making it impossible for me to find any clarity about the issue.

One night, ensconced in my confusion, I thought, "Gee, it sure would be nice if the puppy were closer than four hours away, so I could easily visit to see if her personality is a fit for Sula and me." Less than an hour later, yet another breeder I phoned weeks before called me back to say she had some puppies coming due. She was only forty-five minutes away. Her philosophy was in line with my latest thought. She believed it best if the potential adoptive humans and their pets actually came in person to find the right match. She said that in her years of breeding dogs, prospective buyers who picked a puppy from her Internet photos almost always picked a different puppy when they came to get the one they previously picked.

The coincidences were coalescing around my every changing wish. How was I supposed to decide? As it became increasingly more difficult, I thought, "Gee, I sure wish Sula just had a playmate, so I didn't need to make a decision about another dog."

The next morning when I was outside with Sula, a woman with a small dog walked in front of my home. Her dog was about the same size as Sula. As she and I exchanged courteous chitchat, our dogs began to play. We concluded our exchange with the agreement to get our dogs together periodically for play dates. I was spooked by the coincidences that mimicked my every whim. My dilemma was yet to be resolved because I was not at peace, no matter what form life took around the issue, no matter what "signs" came to me.

The Red Sea parted and acquiesced to my every desire, but each new event brought the sea back together, flooding me emotionally.

The only thing becoming clear was that the situation was less about Sula's needs and more about my own. The emotions I felt were reminiscent of love relationships, where I believed I was under the spell of something larger than I could control.

Rather than relinquish my power to my emotions, I decided to follow them to their source, which was unsuccessful, because my observation was from the position of a spectator watching a tennis match. Immersed in a volley of intellect and desire, I was anything but detached. Each time my intellect served logic, my desire rallied an emotional plea. I knew what I had to do. I called the breeder to let her know I would not be able to take Butterfly. The day was cloudy, which mimicked the cloud of sadness I felt.

I entered into some rite of passage, not when I let go of the decision to get a puppy, but when I allowed myself to feel the sadness around letting go of the decision. Every time I attempt to fill the emptiness inside of me from the outside, I fill the hole before something more can manifest on its own from that emptiness. Through the emptiness, we allow our Spirit's expression to come into creation through our soul pattern, not our unconscious whims. Our soul's creation is not about emotions, but openness to the emptiness beyond emotions when the ripples of emotion cease.

We are creators, and the level from which we create determines the outcome. While a puppy may not sound life threatening, we each have only so much energy. If we squander it in fulfillment of unconscious needs that manifest as something we believe can be resolved with our intellect and emotions, we stay in a repetitive loop that repeats the past. Even if the experience takes a different form, it will follow the same theme. Filling emptiness with a group, relationship, or puppy provides the same distraction. I follow a distinct pattern of taking on more than I can comfortably handle, to avoid my emptiness. The added burden of another dog during a time I was already too busy is an example. Although in this case, the new dog was the pawn. Too much energy was expended in the tangled state of ambivalence trying to decide—the actual distraction. Until the dust settles, we are not able to be impressed from soul-level consciousness, where life is guided by natural synchronicities, not the ones we have created from intellect and desire.

As Joseph Campbell said, "We must be willing to get rid of the life we planned, so as to have the life that is waiting for us."

The optimal function of consciousness is not in the division. The tug-of-war between our attachments and our potential prevents a synthesis. A synthesis is formed by disciplining our conscious mind not to give into our emotional reactions, where we are following our unconscious intent. Letting go of attachments clears the way for a state of balance, where the real magic occurs. From a balanced state, there is no lesson to learn. Our synchronicities are flawless, because our Spirit's intent comes through the soul pattern appropriate for its expression.

About a week after the trial and tribulation of my dog issue, right about the time I absorbed the message it bestowed upon me, I received a call from the woman with the little dog requesting a play date. We met at a local park where the bugs were having more fun biting us than the dogs were having with each other. I offered my house, where they would have the added benefit of Sula's toys. One conversation led to the next, and before I realized the oddness of what occurred, I was watching both dogs at my house while the woman ran off to Costco. It happened so quickly that I didn't even consider the strangeness of it until she was gone and her dog was going crazy from separation anxiety.

I called her to say, "Hey, this isn't going to work out." Her voicemail answered. I called again and again. In the midst of my frantic effort to catch the woman before she had gone too far, my mother called and convinced me the woman strategically found her dog a permanent home and wasn't coming back. The thought that I was stuck with the stranger's neurotic dog filled me with anxiety. I spent the next ten minutes luring and chasing her dog to read its tag to find out where she lived, but the only information engraved on its tag was the same number I had been calling.

Eventually the woman returned for her dog. Needless to say, the play-date idea came to a screeching halt. About the same time, the hawk that coveted my back yard disappeared. Sula and I ventured into the yard, at first apprehensively, but now it's like old times.

As far as a second dog goes, when I reach the point when time permits and my intention is not a means to avoid emptiness, a second dog will be fun. Until then, the temptation to sell out to the illusion will be huge, and, as I found, once I attach my energy to that illusion, many opportunities will be created to invite me to believe it was meant to be. If I am using my intellect and emotions to decipher those opportunities, they were created from the level of my unconscious, and I have squeezed out the soul level of consciousness.

Once a stage play closes, the props for it are no longer needed. Could it be that the props that instigate our experiences are much the same? We worry about the events that unfold before us, yet they are nothing more than a story we tell with a theme. The difference is that rather than read the stories, we act them out.

WHERE THE RUBBER
MEETS THE ROAD

O nce upon a time there was a woman named Susanne who traveled internationally for work. During her travels she befriended a restaurateur and amazing cook. Because she couldn't pronounce his five-syllable Greek last name, he was Stavros to Suzanne long before they became good friends. The first-name basis had no reflection of the respect she felt toward the simple man. From the moment they met, Suzanne recognized the wealth of wisdom he acquired from navigating through a difficult life. Where Suzanne was educated in the finest ivy league schools, her Greek friend never stepped foot in any school. Their lives were polar opposites in every obvious way, but any time he told her a story, it always left her contemplating the deeper meaning he intended for her to find. The significant theme was appropriate for any issue she grappled to resolve, either personally or professionally. Private about her affairs, Suzanne never bogged him down with any of those details, yet he still knew.

Stavros owned a small café she stumbled onto during her first business trip to Athens, Greece. Since then, she secretly conjured reasons to visit her accounts in Athens. Equal to enjoying his company, she craved Stavros's cooking, her favorite being his pastitsio, Greek lasagna.

She teased him that she wanted the recipe so she could open a Greek restaurant like his in America. He would dramatically reply in his broken English, "No, my Susanna, Americana's no enjoy good food. They too busy working."

Quickly she retorted, "Okay, Stavros, just give me the recipe so I can make it for myself."

"No, Susanna, I cannot give; it is my father's recipe he got from my papo, who got from his father, on and on, way back. It is secret family recipe passed down."

Every time they saw each other, they went through the same exchange. It became their ritual, like a secret password, that opened the evening to hours of conversation between the two friends.

The Athens office was under her jurisdiction, so under normal circumstances, she visited at least once a quarter. If Suzanne hadn't had a business trip to Athens in more than three months, she turned into a micro manager and found any excuse to meet with the company's European sales force there. Circumstances were anything but normal, and it had been well past six months since her last trip to Athens. She was in the midst of a divorce and all the life changes that coincide with the end of a ten-year marriage. Her situation took its toll on her normally confident and self-assured persona. Suzanne's self-esteem plummeted from the moment she found out her husband was having an affair. Reluctantly she planned to go after being summoned by the Athens office to be part of a major presentation. Heading to her favorite country didn't lift Suzanne's spirits.

The Athens office wasn't expecting her until the next day, so an early arrival gave her time to acclimate. The long flight didn't stop a tired Suzanne from seeing her friend, once she landed. Her first order of business, even before checking into her hotel, was a cab ride to his restaurant.

As soon as she walked in, Stavros could tell she was not herself. It had been her birthday two days before, but he knew her birthday was not the issue. Over the seven years that he had known Suzanne, he had seen her on many birthday weeks, and she always took aging in stride. Not missing a beat, he went and got his private stash of ouzo and shared a drink with her. They talked for a while.

Desperately she wanted to share with Stavros what she was feeling, but she knew she would not be able to stop crying if she talked about it. Without any direct conversation of her problems, he offered her great comfort. In his presence she felt genuinely cared for.

When she was leaving, he handed her a piece of baklava for her to enjoy later and an envelope. It was not unusual for him to send her off with food, but she was touched that this time he gave her a birthday card.

Less than forty-eight hours later, after a whirlwind of meetings, Suzanne was on a flight back to the States. Sipping on some water, she glanced out the window. The downtime on the flight brought her personal life back into focus, and the emotional pain of her pending divorce engulfed her. She remembered the card Stavros gave her and pulled it from her purse. She knew any card from him would make her smile, but to her surprise, it was not a card at all. It was his recipe. For the rest of the flight, time stood still. She forgot all her cares and rode home higher than the clouds the plane broke through. Elated, all she thought about was where she would get the ingredients, supplies, and preparatory tools to make the best pastitsio. She was going to make his lineage proud.

Back home, she wore herself out running throughout Atlanta to find the freshest herbs, the finest imported olive oil from Greece, the most exquisite pasta maker, the perfect pan, and everything else she needed.

Two days of prepping and cooking led to the magical moment. Suzanne pulled the beautiful pastitsio from the oven, tossed her Greek salad, and poured a glass of Greek wine to accompany the delightful entrée she was about to eat. She smiled as she savored the smell, which immediately took her back to Stavros's restaurant. The look on her face was of someone about to indulge in a joyful, bon appetite moment. "This one is for you, Stavros," she said with the first bite. Her look changed drastically. "What happened?" It did not taste the same as Stavros's. She couldn't understand what she did wrong. Surely he would not have tricked her. She sipped her wine while a tear streamed down her face. She had not make his lineage proud.

Several more months passed before Suzanne was back in Athens. As usual, her first order of business was seeing Stavros. While he was heating up her favorite meal, she told him in detail of her failure, to which he responded, "My Susanna, you left out main ingredient."

"But how could I have left anything out? I followed all your directions. I did everything you told me to."

"Ah," he said, "no one in my family follow recipe. Recipe for monkey. You left out most important ingredient. Yourself."

Each of us is unique. As a result, the products we produce, the relationships we form, and the life we live is unique to us. If we could see that uniqueness with awe rather than feeling disenfranchised by the mold we can't fit, our lives would mean much more.

My first-grade teacher, Mrs. Vanarski, shared a concept with my class that I never considered. It became a profound moment that, like a tattoo, left a permanent mark on my psyche.

On a snowy winter morning, Mrs. Vanarski shifted us from math class to art class with out-of-character enthusiasm. She began by telling my class that no two snowflakes were alike. "We are each like the different-shaped snowflakes that are falling outside the window," she exclaimed. "No two people are alike." She talked us through the assignment to prove it. She told us to make our own snowflake out of white construction paper. She showed us how to fold the paper and then randomly cut into it with our scissors. Since we had to wait for each student to finish before we could unfold the paper, our excitement mounted into a frenzy. Those of us who finished first could barely wait for the slow pokes. Once every student was finished, together we unveiled the completed works of art. Unfolded, the paper revealed the unmistakable result. Lo and behold, she was right! No two patterns were alike, not even close.

On the cusp of the age of reason and spellbound by the discovery, I never noticed she contradicted her lesson with one gesture. While I worked, my tongue was pressed against my upper lip, Mrs. Vanarski came over and took my scissors out of my left hand and put them into my right hand. She often had to remind me to be right handed like the majority, versus being left handed, which was my natural inclination.

Years later I found out that the analogy Mrs. Vanarski shared, that we are each like snowflakes, separate and unique, was a borrowed, worn-out cliché. Like all clichés, lip service is paid to the meaning, but they are rarely followed by action. Preoccupied with fitting in, we allow the distinctions that separate us to melt. As we focus on being accepted, we dampen our uniqueness until we can't identify what separates us. Like the individual snowflakes that are mashed together to construct a snowball, we are no longer identifiable individually.

Did you know that snowflakes are actually particles carried into the atmosphere by the wind? Under certain weather conditions, ice forms around these particles, creating the snowflake we actually see. Particles enter the atmosphere already unique and separate, and the weather accentuates and decorates them.

With that tidbit of knowledge, I considered my personality characteristics and those first experiences that highlighted them.

When my mother called "Sofia," rather than my nickname, in a voice that bordered on hysteria, I knew I was in trouble. One story I remember, because my pride was not outdone by the trouble I got in, was the day Mrs. Shamento, a tattletale neighbor, called my mother when she saw me selling the same flowers on the corner that were missing from her garden. Quick on my feet, I had a good reason. My response was, "The flowers were almost dead, and I wanted other people to see them before they died." Okay, that answer may not impress you, but I was five at the time. By the way, I made eighty-five cents that day as an early entrepreneur.

I was a sensitive child, and my two older sisters enjoyed exploiting that trait. One of their favorite pastimes was playing dead in front of me. I would cry over their play-dead bodies until they couldn't hold in their laughter any longer. Between their gasps for air while laughing, they usually called me names like "sucker" or "loser," because I fell for it every time. Two against one, I was outnumbered.

Even though I could parrot the saying "Sticks and stones can break my bones, but names will never hurt me," I always felt hurt. My ability to strategize overcompensated for my sensitivity, however. While my sisters fought with mere words, I eventually used my camera to gather evidence for blackmail. My photo ops took place anytime they were doing what my mother didn't permit, such as kissing a boy.

By the contrast to my sisters' interests, I discovered some of my likes and dislikes early. My sisters were always playing with dolls.

Since I wanted to be with them, I went along with stupid dolls. They would spend half a day dressing up their dolls for a ball all the dolls were attending. Mine, on the other hand, came waltzing in without any clothes. I always had a good reason, such as "Their clothes were in the wash." Since I got stuck with the special-needs dolls, the ones missing legs or arms, it was quite a sight. Eventually they retired their special-needs dolls, and I was no longer invited to play.

As a child I spent a significant amount of time alone watching and observing life. Where one may conclude that I became a loner because my sisters rejected me, I say I was far too determined to be easily rejected, and I enjoyed processing life by observation.

When my father came to visit, he told us tales to justify his absence. He was always working hard on business. I often challenged him on the discrepancies of his stories, like an attorney questioning a witness on trial. My oldest sister would get angry at me for disagreeing with him, and I would say, "But he is lying." When he missed paying his child support, I would look him squarely in the eyes and boldly ask, "Why didn't you pay Mom?" My search for truth, and the desire to hold others accountable, was as much a part of my existence then as it is now.

My mother used to say, "People don't change." I not only disagreed, but I was vehement with my argument. As an adult, those three words my mother spoke frequently play back in my mind, but I no longer reject them with the accusatory anger of a naïve child. Rather than hear judgment, I revere her words as a sprinkle of wisdom from a woman who has lived longer than I.

Life experience may reshape our outlook. The body that encircles us may submit to age, but our personality, as the interface between the force of our Spirit and form of our body, is the medium that enables us to interact in the physical world, and it doesn't change. How we direct the use of our personality may change, but who we are remains the same.

Similarly, the ingredients that go into recipes are the same for any recipe. For instance, sugar is sweet and salt is bitter. We can influence the taste of what we are cooking by how much or how little we add. A cookie would taste odd if we added more salt than sugar, and a roast would taste wrong if it had too much sugar. How we influence our world doesn't depend on our personality as much as how we pour ourselves into any given moment. Tenacity is a good personality trait for a stroke survivor, but not for an adult trying to change another adult.

Birthright

Three children can be born and raised in the same household by the same set of parents and display more differences than similarities. Perplexed at how different from each other my sisters and I were, I read the characteristics associated with birth order, in an effort to gain some understanding. Around that same time, I dated a twin who was easygoing and fun-loving. I was excited to meet the other twin, expecting it would mean an instant friendship. Instead I was shocked by the difference in their personalities. Where the one I dated was likeable and lighthearted, the other was by the same degree difficult and intense. They were mirror opposites of each other. How could that be, when they were born minutes apart and raised in the same family? Fascinated by all the contrasts, I paged through my birth order book, where there was a caveat for twins. It suggested the minimal time difference of their birth was enough to have an effect on their personalities and make them different.

Like blanket-statement horoscopes intended to apply to every person born under a particular sign, the psychological profiles identified by birth order were laced with loopholes forgiving enough to permit the siblings of any family to fit into any category, regardless of birth order, even justifying the difference in twins by the minutes separating their birth. Vagueness made the information lose validity, making the book useful only for fun. While I poke at the premise behind the theory of birth order, it is one among many psychological theories that lend logic but don't make sense beyond face value. No matter which theory I subscribed to, there was always that caveat lurking behind the premise, waiting to be discovered, nullifying the whole. Coming from a real estate background where contracts easy to nullify were considered weak agreements, I find all-encompassing theories weak when they attempt to explain who we are yet include a nullifying clause. When will specialists realize we don't fit in tidy boxes?

Could it be the missing link to solidify the mysteries in life is not missing at all, but pulled apart from our need to harmonize our characteristics with one lifetime? The unique formula of Spirit contained by consciousness or soul that begets our expression is a combination of experience and lifetimes that form the chemistry that defines who we are prior to birth. While there are theories that aid our understanding of the components that make up the psyche, they eliminate the living force that occupies the psyche in each incarnation.

"Our Greatest Blessing is Our Curse"

The current incarnation is the fertile ground compatible with where the last one ended, so that we can take root to continue our evolution. The characteristics evidenced in youth are not an accident. They are orchestrated to perfection so that we can bring into creation the unique expression of our eternal Spirit. Life provides us the opportunities to refine those personality characteristics so that we are able to manifest our purpose. Our personality is the touchstone for manifestation. Karma, or the lessons we are indebted to, is a way for us to refine the personality to bring forth our essence.

Going back to the story of the time when I made money from the neighbor's flowers, if you knew I was raised without money and saw the hardship on my mother, who struggled to support her three daughters and herself on a sales clerk income, you might conclude I was determined to make money not only to avoid replicating her struggles, but also to help her. I choose to say that I came into this incarnation full of determination, and my response to my childhood was where my determination was first made apparent, just like the weather does not create the particles in the atmosphere, but makes them visible as snowflakes.

The predominant characteristics made obvious by my early life experiences are easily identifiable as determined, sensitive, strategic, observant, and wrapped up with an innate tendency to strive toward truth and accountability. You may think those characteristics are good, and from there you may even conclude my personality could have easily handled age-appropriate life challenges well. Our characteristics are in themselves neutral, though. How we express them in relation to our experiences gives them meaning. Witnessed through my experiences, my greatest character assets were also my biggest liabilities.

I abided by an unrealistic work ethic, and my determination nearly killed me. My determination combined with my observant nature can sear straight to the point, and often people interpret that directness as aggressive and judgmental. My demand for truth and accountability has funneled into self-righteousness. My sensitivity makes relationships difficult, when it is projected through criticism or defensiveness. My strategic nature can provoke obsessive thinking. The other side of the coin conjures my determination as the reason for my success in any endeavor I undertake, while I strategically carve my path. My boldness is an asset to help me maneuver through the bureaucracy of life, which otherwise makes us subservient to the dictates of any system, regardless of our rights and what is right. My search for truth and accountability motivates me to help others navigate life easier, and helps me navigate life easier as well. My sensitivity and keen observation allow me to see through my motives and empathize with others. I understand the pain their unconscious promptings cause.

The duality of our personality is our blessing and curse. A dog trainer unknowingly clarified the tangled terrain of the psyche for me. During agility class, while the instructor taught the best technique for a particular series of obstacles, she said, "Since you don't know which dog you will be running on which day, it is best to be positioned where you cover all bases."

Trying to comprehend her words literally, I asked, "What do you mean, which dog? Of course I will be running Sula."

The instructor answered, "You never know where your dog will be in any moment…fast, slow, distracted, or whatever." I got it, but more in regard to the human experience.

A constant sifting and sorting occurs within. We are a matrix built from experiences, combined with our propensity to process them. At any given moment, we don't know what part of us is going to float to the surface and have the most influence or why.

Anyone who has ever experienced insomnia has a glimpse of traveling through the rough terrain of the psyche without ever leaving bed. In the quiet darkness, the monsters that lurked in our childhood closets take residence in our adult mind. Our dream state goes deeper into the tangled terrain of the unconscious, but uses the language of symbols we don't consciously understand. In the light of day, even the worst nightmare quickly fades in significance, because we can't decipher the language of our inner battle.

A part of our character surfaces to meet the experience that will polish it. Our Waterloo is at the height of incongruence between what is being demanded of us from the experience and how we apply our personality to the situation. When we cannot appropriately connect our personality with something that is demanded of us, it appears we met our downfall. What we have really met is an undeveloped part of our character ready to be developed.

Sandra's husband used a cash advance on their credit cards to pay for household expenses. Unknown to Sandra, he ran up debt faster than he could cover it. He rationalized the secret by his intention to pay the debt. The jobs and income he needed didn't come in as planned, though. What he thought was a temporary financial downturn festered into a critical financial wound he could no longer conceal from his wife. The incident almost cost the family their home. Sandra was devastated by the ordeal. Once they refinanced their home, taking cash back from the equity to pay off the debt, the responsibilities of a busy life conveniently aided her ability to bury the deeper issues in her marriage beneath the surface

Almost two years later, Sandra was in a women's networking group and recounted to her friend Beverly how she didn't feel compatible with the other women in the group. She said, "You wouldn't believe it; two of them date men who run up their charge cards and don't carry their financial weight, and the women are too disempowered to realize they have no support from their partners, financial or otherwise. I have nothing in common with them; they are young and stupid."

"Out of sight, out of mind" doesn't apply to the issues we don't face. The psyche eventually brings them to the surface for completion. It is part of the refinement of our personality. Sandra allotted her husband mercy, but then judged harshly the other women who did the same thing. Her sensitivity is usually her strength when she relates to others or, in this case, it became a critical barrier to avoid facing herself. The difficulties in her marriage were not a collection of minor annoyances, such as someone leaving the toilet seat up, leaving clothes on the floor, or frequently running late. The issues exploded into difficulties symbolic of trusting another at the expense of losing herself.

Psychology refers to the super-ego, which overlays the personality. Carl Jung referred to it as the personal unconscious. However it is labeled, it is the junction where the personality is introduced and influenced by the world of "should," without which it would be difficult to interact with the outer environment. The downside is that rather than tempering our true nature with the outer environment, the ego is swayed by its attachment to the outer environment, so it accommodates that attachment, while our true nature is left to flounder, never building the strength of character to bring forth the expression of our Spirit.

I grew up in the North during a time where the technology of four-wheel drive was limited to the vehicles that plowed the roads after a snowstorm. The rest of us had snow tires. Ours were in the form of a chain apparatus put around our regular tires each winter. When the weather shifted to spring, the snow chains were the first thing we removed. The fine imposed for damaging the roads discouraged procrastination. There was a date set for when the rubber had to meet the road.

The personality projection as the outermost reflection of who we are is where the rubber meets the road in our life. Our personality, applied appropriately, allows the expression of our Spirit to touch manifestation. Conditioned by norms, compensatory behaviors, instinctual reflexes, and our defenses, we become bound by self-imposed chains that surpass helpful and become hurtful. If the cost in life were only a meager fine, eagerly we would wait in line to write the check.

SPINNING THE WHEEL OF LIFE

One of the most frustrating moments in life is when we are misunderstood. If words were an entity in themselves, we would hear the word *ego* complain about how it is often misrepresented and misused. The term "ego demolishment" has become a popular concept held in high regard and honored by many modern teachings. It is a term frequently tossed around, but understood by few. It has been coined as a catch-all phrase to label a behavior, rather than reflect on the behavior to unravel the meaning of what occurred. Just the other day, when I asked a friend how she was doing with a significant conflict that erupted between a family member and her, her response was, "As soon as I saw that my ego got in the way, I became okay with the situation." There it was again, used like an empty shell, warranting no further self-reflection. I had a vision of my friend sweeping the issue, a real problem, under the rug she swiftly weaved out of the word *ego*. I didn't know who to feel sorrier for, my friend or the misunderstood word.

The ego has been a necessary part of our evolving conscious-ness; why the sudden urgency to destroy it? Without ego we would be left in a zombie-like state, because the ego is the realization of one's self. A child awakens his ego the moment he recognizes he is separate from his surroundings, including his parents. The child's effort to define himself is accomplished from the contrast of who he is against who he is not. In the process of individualizing, he finds an outer identity he wants to become. The hero he mimics becomes less specific as he matures.

I watched my nephew go from being Bob the Builder to Spi-derman to Batman, and so on. Each year his alias was different. At ten years old, he was a professional wrestler by his association as a spectator. Enthralled with entertainment wrestling, he lived for permission to watch it on television, and he recited the names and titles of most wrestlers as well as sports commentators. By the time we are adults, our identity becomes an interwoven conglomerate of our heroes and our personal goals. It isn't as single-focused as a child's, but our identity, like the child's, is usually in association with something outside of us. The desire to demolish the little realization we have of ourselves, though, even if it is at the level of a child's consciousness, is not the solution to gain self-realization.

I grew up close to an amusement park. My favorite game was spin-ning a huge wheel that pointed to a random prize. The prizes ranged from worthless trinkets all the way up to stuffed animals that towered over my slight, child-sized stature. Each time I took my turn, I mus-tered up as much momentum as I could with my spin, but the wheel always stopped short of the prize I wanted. Our lives are not much different from the amusement park game. We spin the wheel called life with high hopes that if we spin it just right, we can get it to land on the prize, the prize we are certain will add meaning to existence. It goes something like this: If I am thinner, he'll ask me out. If I accumulate more wealth, she'll marry me. If I work harder, they'll promote me. After he asks her out, she realizes they have little in common. After she marries him, he believes it is his money she is after. After she gets the promotion, she longs for her old, less-stressful job.

We associate our identity to an outer attachment sure to give our life meaning, such as relationships, status, job, money, a house, and so on, down the endless list. Our real attachment is not to the thing, but what the thing represents to us. My attachment to my house is not to the physicality of the space, but to how I feel when I am in my house, how I feel when I drive down my street, and how I feel when someone comes over and compliments my house. Something then goes wrong. Rainwater gets into the garage because the driveway has settled. All of the sudden, what made me happy is costing me grief, time, and money. There is never any warning when something will appear and be the other side of what we derive our satisfaction from. We are left experiencing dissatisfaction, equally as intense. My house is a contrast between joy and hardship.

The physical world is an intricate web of duality. We struggle against the immutable law of action in the physical world, where we eventually go through both sides of each experience, while our ego lands wherever the momentum ceases. We're on top of the world one day and lower than insects the following day. Since the physical world is under the jurisdiction of opposites, the force of life plays out in an interrelated drama of opposing forms, beneath the illusion they are separate. Reality, as it definitively appears, is a temporary movement from one side of the spectrum, until momentum builds to push back in the other direction.

From, *Letters of Helena Roerich, volume 2,* "The great Buddha, when selecting disciples, used to test them on their ability to contain, as it were, pairs of opposites. If a disciple could not master this, Buddha would not advance him to further knowledge, since this not only would be useless, but harmful as well. The awareness of reality is achieved only by way of perpetual change and confrontation of pairs of opposites."

We must cease to focus on the narrow state of consciousness in the outer world in search of inner meaning from what is temporal by design. For instance, hastily we run from one form because we blame it on how we feel in the present and seek refuge. There is no refuge. Each experience is the opposite of a sum total, broken apart for us to absorb each half of the whole. We realize a broadened consciousness when we derive inner meaning rather than form an allegiance to impermanence. The friction from the collision of the opposites produces a healthy discomfort. It is a barometer that alerts us when we have formed symbiosis with an aspect of the outer world the same as a virus does when it finds the perfect host.

Where Amy's energy would be better used running 5K races, Amy runs from what she perceives as negative feelings. To her detriment, she has perfected her ability to attract attention. Some people have a contagious laugh. When you hear them laugh, regardless of how funny the joke or incident, you can't help laughing with them. Amy's personality is like that. It is contagious, and no matter where she is, whatever she is doing, if other people are around, they want to be in her presence. Sadly for this jovial woman, she has a disease often referred to as "the grass is always greener on the other side." The friendships she maintains change often. In her case, since the pickings are never slim, there is rarely a lull between BFFs. One week her best friend forever may be Lisa; the next week, Lisa falls out of glory, and Amy forms a new allegiance to Beth. Amy picks and chooses her allegiance by what she feels in the moment, and if it is fondness toward someone, usually the person is reflecting to her what she wants to see in herself. As most people, the chosen friend enamored by Amy exhibits awe in her presence. When the newly formed friendship comes down to daily living, Amy's interpretation of any human frailty in her friend is her friend's fall from grace. For example, Amy shares gossip with that friend, and the friend shares it with someone else. Amy labels the friend a gossip, and shortly thereafter ends the friendship. As if she had a magic wand, she poofs that individual out of her life and is on to the next spontaneous attachment. There is never any time to form a lasting, loving friendship that comes with knowing someone on a deeper level, because Amy's relationship within herself is fleeting.

She changes jobs with the same frequency as she changes friends. Because of her personality, regardless of how tight the job market is, she finds a well-paying job, even though she is not as qualified as other interviewees. The people who hire her are usually swept away by her charisma. It then comes time to work, and the admiration from her employer translates in her mind to demands. Her resignation follows shortly thereafter.

The contrast of what feels good against when it doesn't is not life's malicious moment, but its generosity. Life gracefully moves us from pain to sorrow by the degree we need to experience the contrast. Life is not a pursuit of pleasure, but a blend of pleasure and pain. The pleasure draws us in to experience the lesson the pain instills, to break our attachment. If we go from one experience to the next eking out all that is pleasurable and avoid feeling pain, we indebt ourselves to experiences that provide balance. In Amy's case, she is out of sync with the ebb and flow of life, seeking only the flow. Duality will catch up as a climactic event or happening, forcing her to pause. The contrast is what takes us past our outer attachments and delivers the opportunity to experience inner awareness. When the duality of our experiences collides and the good feeling we had is wrought with sadness, in a sense it is our spiritual offering to God. Whatever moves us to forge a deeper awareness of ourselves increases our connection to God. It is to the extent that we know ourselves that we know the divinity within.

Each time pleasure is nullified by pain, in our disappointment, in our loss, through our tears, after a burst of anger, we seal off another route on the dead-end search and affix a sign that reads: "If you are looking for yourself, do not trespass here." It is a good thing, because the sooner the escape routes are blocked, the sooner we stop running from ourselves.

Because we are resilient, we continue to search for wholeness in the physical world. If we become fixated on something outside ourselves to make us whole, with enough determination, we eventually attain our desire. The attainment of desire is not the wonderment of life; the wonderment is the belief that what we attained in a temporal reality will last. At the precise moment of attainment, we have simultaneously put in an order for the opposite. It is not a warning to stop participating in life, but an explanation of why we often feel defeated by life when we search for fulfillment from without. A broadened consciousness is not like a prize we will win if we spin the wheel of life just right. Instead, broadened consciousness comes from meeting the depth and breadth of our potential through the duality of life. As Carl Jung states, "When an inner situation is not made conscious to us, it appears on the outside as fate."

December 31, 2001, was highlighted on my calendar with a star, but not because it brought forth the promise of a new year, and I had no special plans that New Year's Eve. The date indicated a significant turning point in my life. It was the day I planned to retire my real estate license to soul search. Around that time, I was seeing a psychologist to help me sort out the ending of a significant relationship. In our final session, I shared my upcoming plans and my excitement about the freedom I believed was in arm's reach. She disagreed with me on what I needed, to feel free. She told me that freedom is not about having or not having a career. I politely exited her office with the thought, "She's good about dealing with loss but doesn't know a thing about the demands required of a Realtor."

Each day that passed, I marked off the calendar, leaving fewer days in the way of the sacred date. I planned how I would fill my time once I was free to do what I wanted. Naturally I indulged in planning the events I never had time for, while working. I looked forward to those plans with great anticipation of a wonderful life ahead. When time caught up to the date I eagerly awaited, I was off and running like a horse out of the starting gate. Excited to plunge into my new life, I never looked back. I took trips out of the country. I attended self-help courses. I embarked on many healing modalities, including acupuncture, and I went on spa retreats. It was a dream schedule. I even bought the right candles and music to meditate, now that I had the time. Months later, while I was getting ready for a massage appointment, it occurred to me that in my endeavor to be free, I carried the same burden as a work routine. The meaning of life I believed was hidden because of my real estate career was as elusive in retirement. I felt once again like the child who spun the wheel but missed the prize.

Engulfed in nothingness, I met my match, a new friend who had lost her job. We took long walks every morning and commiserated about the emptiness we felt. We called ourselves the "no-nothing twins," because for the first time, by the force if circumstances, we relinquished control and acknowledged the unknown our future held. Shortly thereafter, she met the man she would marry, and I no longer had a twin. I felt the no-nothingness all alone. No relationship, no job, and I lost my no-nothing friend. I retired from a career that defined who I was; the freedom I longed to find didn't magically appear, and I didn't find the soul I searched for. The date I awaited with high hope didn't change a thing. The eternal happiness I set out to find was missing in the city of freedom I developed—a city unworthy of its name.

Recently I read about a man who was on a wilderness hike and got lost. His plight to find his way was a horrid adventure that lasted days. Right before he was rescued, he felt the most despair, but it was at that moment that he was less than a quarter mile from safety. The more he panicked, the farther he was from locating the destination he frantically sought. He wasn't able to adjust his internal compass with the external world, which nearly killed him. Similarly, it was in hindsight that I discovered I was closer to finding my soul at the moment when I felt most lost. Without the outer identity my career gave me, I wasn't much different from the man lost in the wilderness, because my internal compass and the external world no longer meshed. The closer I was to the meaning I searched, the further away it appeared. The search for inner meaning that I consciously embarked on at the close of 2001 was a continuation of the search I unconsciously had been on my whole life.

My search for meaning began as a child who felt something was missing. There were clues that something existed beyond determined reality, and the clues implied there were different rules, ones we were not privy to in the material world. Sometimes I caught a glimpse of that far-off world through a crack in the door between reality and something more, but I ran when I touched the threshold. There were the ghost stories shared during pajama parties, the sixth sense assigned to the person with extraordinary wisdom, the Ouija board that answered the questions my friends and I asked of fate, the eccentric woman at the carnival who looked at my palm and accurately recited my past as well as predicted my future, the psychic fair that featured a woman whose voice and mannerisms changed as she channeled the spirit of a wise, dead man. Those early curiosities planted a seedling of desire to reach beyond what time and space defined and school books taught.

Once I became an adult, the trepidation I experienced in childhood about the unknown was no longer a desire to explore muted by fear. It morphed into feeling uneasy about the lack of consistency among the theories passed off as truth. Often we are seduced by what seems to touch an inner level, when we are looking for the comfort that we imagine will follow, and unwittingly it only reinforces our attachment to physical existence. When my dog Jeremy was killed, a woman who claimed to communicate with the souls of dead animals assured me that he would reincarnate as another dog in my lifetime. She explained that because pets have such a short life span relative to their humans, they reincarnate—sometimes multiple times—and end up back in our lives as another pet. Desperate to bring back my dog and hopeful by the woman's romantic proposition, I was ready to run out and purchase a puppy born precisely the same day and time Jeremy died. Going to her to gain awareness about a life beyond physical existence, I left more attached to physical existence, clinging to the hope that my dog would return to my life, rather than finding peace around his untimely death.

We collect idealized concepts that not only glorify the people who bring them forward, but also keep us fixed in physical life, while we maintain an illusion we have touched into the spiritual. One day it hits us, our life is no better for it. We still struggle with relationships, decisions, finding our purpose, and so forth. We are no different from the ones who are convinced that if they amass enough of something in the material world, life will be better. Either drama plays out the same; life's a struggle, life has no meaning, life is pain.

A good detective doesn't abandon the murder scene laden with clues if he hasn't solved the crime. The scene of the crime is where he begins to extract all possible evidence. Unlike a detective solving a mystery, we become scattered when we search in all directions to seek solace and meaning beyond the confines of the physical world. It is customary for people to make the leap from the physical world to the spiritual, expecting to be caught in a net of understanding. We cannot clothe ourselves in God by following a spiritual practice, new age teaching, or religious belief, any more than my nephew could become Batman when clothed in a Halloween costume. The best we can hope for is to bring God to our human experience.

A developed consciousness is the bridge, with the potential of bringing heaven to earth, where we are receptive to our Spirit, divinity, or God within. We support the bridge between heaven and earth each time we broaden consciousness, and we weaken it when we narrow consciousness. With each experience in the outer world where we extract inner meaning, we broaden consciousness. When we identify with the experience, we reinforce our attachment to the outer world, narrowing consciousness.

Building a Bridge between Heaven and Earth

Math was one of my favorite subjects in school. Where math is cut and dried, I found zero to be math's anomaly. By itself zero meant *nothing*, but behind a number, it is a different story and means a lot. The more zeros behind a number means even more. My odd intrigue with zero is similar to my understanding of the intellect. How we use it determines whether it adds meaning to our life. The expression of our intellect determines the strength of the foundation for the bridge where we bring heaven to earth. A narrow consciousness is our intellect crawling on earth, being directed by our animal nature, versus walking upright directed by our soul, where we are receptive to any impression from our Spirit.

Anyone who has trained a dog knows successful training involves incremental, repetitive, redirecting behavior. Humans have the same animal nature, but where a dog's is guided by instinct, our animal nature is guided by intellect.

For instance, an ambulance drove by with its siren on. I was less startled by the sound than I was by my dog, Sula. She howled. I never heard her howl, so I was both amazed and amused. Her twelve-pound body let out a howl normally associated with her much larger ancestors in the wild. I was reminded of the oddity several months later. On our normal walk through the neighborhood, a fire truck passed as it headed in the direction of an emergency. Sula howled until the sound of the siren was far off in the distance. Intrigued to find out why sirens caused her to respond with a howl, I researched the strange occurrence. I found it is not unusual for domestic dogs to display behaviors of their ancestors, regardless of whether those behaviors have merit in the life of a household pet. For instance, the sound of a siren becomes associated with the sound of a lone wolf separated from his pack. The howl is a call to say, "I am here, where are you?" The nearest wolf howls back to say, "Over here." Its intellect is governed by an instinct that has no usefulness to the domesticated dog, incapable of reasoning, "Hey, that is a siren; I don't need to follow the impulse of my animal nature and respond to it."

Similarly, when I let a guest in my home, I am very careful to make sure at the moment the guest enters, the dog doesn't exit. My street is not terribly busy, but the few cars that pass my house whiz by at twice the posted speed limit. Since there is a sidewalk across the street, people often pass on foot, and often with a dog in tow. Sula believes she has domain over her area, so my concern is that Sula could see a dog and protectively dart out across the street, barking. She lacks the intellect to reason, "Hmmm, if I run toward that poodle, I could get crushed by several tons of steel before I reach it."

As mankind, we pride ourselves on our intellect, but often it is pulled by the animal nature of our unconscious mind, much like a dog on a leash pulling his master. It is easier to spot domination of the animal nature in someone else than it is to see it in ourselves, because when we are pulled by our animal nature, we are moving too fast and furiously to focus on anything else.

When people in a crowd trample over others to be the first to purchase merchandise on sale, is that situation much different then animals in the wild that will kill whatever gets in the way of food?

What about the father who doesn't agree with a call his son's Little League coach made and starts a fight that ends in murder? How different is that situation from animals in the wild that will kill to protect their young?

Consider the senior citizen bridge team that pushes out the weakest player. No longer able to engage in the game and the social contact that stimulated her mind, she goes off to die on her own. How different is that from animals in the wild that kill the weakest in the pack?

Often the intellect is used in collusion with the animal nature, and that's when we become clever and cunning. Rather than react to the outer world, we try to manipulate it, and in the process justify actions we would otherwise judge another harshly over.

Repeatedly, the truck drivers in training were told that safety comes first. Joe had the highest score in his truck-driving class. He was the smartest trainee, and his new manager felt lucky to have Joe as a new hire. After completing a battery of classes and tests, Joe was ready to drive the rig on the open road. Before sunrise he masterfully directed it toward a town hundreds of miles from home. By dusk, Joe felt confident behind the wheel of the massive truck he had maneuvered all day without a hitch, so when he received a text message from his girlfriend, he didn't hesitate to respond. Because he and his girlfriend were separated by the distance he drove, Joe became mesmerized by the text exchange while driving. He could recite the page number and paragraph of the training manual that emphasized text messaging was prohibited. He knew he should keep his eyes on the road, but he felt deprived; it was the first night he spent alone since he met his girlfriend two months earlier. He figured out a system where he could both text and drive. Between each word he read or typed, he managed a sweeping glance of the road. "Just one more exchange," he thought. While reading that last text message, he missed the sudden change of speed of the car in front of him.

In another scenario, Beverly and a fellow coworker were the two most likely candidates to fill the spot when their manager retired at the end of the year. During a joint sales call with the regional manager who was involved in the decision, Beverly nonchalantly mentioned she was concerned about her coworker. Once she had the regional manager's attention, she exaggerated her coworker's distraction over a pending divorce. She voiced it as concern, but the only thing Beverly was concerned about was getting the promotion.

Our animal nature, as it dominates our intellect, or our intellect, as it supports our animal nature in the process of attainment, short circuits consciousness, because the focus becomes fixed on the narrow state of consciousness where we seek identification from what we have: the success of our children, who we know, a belief we confirm, what we do, how good we are at what we do, and so on. Eventually, as a circuit breaker trips because more power is demanded of it than it can handle, the narrow state of consciousness into which our outer attainment is plugged fails. Our children make a mistake, someone we admire disappoints us, the belief we cherish is challenged, someone else does what we do better, and so on. When we limit our expression to obtainment in the outer world, we constrict consciousness and indulge our animal nature.

People have tamed wild animals. The longstanding Vegas act of Siegfried and Roy was a prime example of tamed animals, until their tiger, Montecore, almost killed Roy. The incident began when an audience member overestimated the domestication of the animal and created a commotion. When Montecore headed toward the noise, Roy desperately tried to regain the tiger's attention. He knew better than to trust the animal that was suddenly enthralled with the audience. Unfortunately Roy tripped during that part of the act he had not practiced, and Montecore reacted instinctually by carrying his tamer off to safety, like he would a cub, by the neck.

Our animal nature is not domesticated. We may have it tamed, but anytime we identify with something outside of us, we create a commotion, and there is no telling how our animal nature will respond, potentially jeopardizing our safety and the safety of those around us.

Our animal nature has a purpose. It is essential for building the foundation for the bridge that brings heaven to earth, if we learn to incrementally and repetitively redirect its behavior. We redirect our animal nature first by using the strength of our animal nature for the discipline needed to detach from drama. The desire of our animal nature, as the motor behind our drive, must be directed away from pursuing outer identification and redirected to an unyielding determination to uncover our true essence. The endurance of our animal nature must be directed away from controlling outcomes and redirected to accepting that what is brought before us is what we need to grow. The courage of our animal nature must be directed away from following others and redirected in a way that defines our individual convictions and takes action based on them. The survival instinct of our animal nature must be directed away from our fear of death and redirected into a belief in the continuity of life, with karma as our guide.

THE SHADOW OF CANCER

Every human being is the author of his own health or disease.
—Buddha

Greek mythology has variations of the story about a centaur named Chiron, who is often referred to as the wounded healer. Chiron, like all centaurs, was half man, half beast, but he was different from most centaurs in that he didn't recklessly indulge his senses. Where other centaurs displayed behaviors leading to intoxication and lust, which usually precipitated violence, Chiron's manner was civilized and kind. The rumor that might explain the contrast is that Chiron was a descendant of a god. The legend further describes Chiron as a gifted teacher of medicine. He even taught medicine to other gods. It was said that Zeus was one of his students.

One fateful day Chiron was seemingly in the wrong place at the wrong time and was wounded by a poisonous arrow. If one believed in accidents, it easily could have been labeled an accident, since the archer didn't intend to aim in Chiron's direction. Had Chiron not been immortal, the severe wound certainly would have killed him. He wished for his own death, because the pain was more intense than he could tolerate. It sent him into the center of the earth howling in agony. Not until he reached the point of total despair, with no way out, was he able to heal. Healing was the transformation that expanded his world, which sounds odd, since he already seemed to have found his purpose in life. It wasn't until he had to heal himself that he became a healer for others. Where his gift of teaching medicine was useful, he ultimately understood the limitations of medicine and the infiniteness of healing. Until then, he was not ready for his true calling. Fate nudged him through the natural propensity of his expression, but other than that, fate patiently waited.

One of my favorite quotes by Carl Jung summarizes the myth of Chiron in two sentences: "The doctor is effective only when he himself is affected. Only the wounded physician heals."

When we heal ourselves, that healed place in us becomes a conduit that reaches the inner wound of another. It transfers a soothing energy that offers a respite from pain, like the salve that soothes a flesh wound. Sometimes the break, regardless of the length of the break, makes us aware that there is another option to suffering. We have all had the experience of feeling comforted in another's presence without a logical reason to justify the feeling, since there was nothing exceptional about what the person said or did. It could have been someone we met in passing, like the person behind us in line who generously shares a warm smile.

Over time the neglected inner wound often manifests physically through disease, but the source of poison feeding the wound is not physical. When the physical symptoms are gone, there is a false sense of relief that circulates around the word *remission*. Remission is not synonymous with *cured*. It describes the resting cycle of disease. True healing comes after we have touched the core of the inner wound. Until we heal from the inside out, we have a crack in our foundation that serves as a reservoir containing poisonous concepts that contradict our true nature. The absence of inner growth creates a stagnant pool of old truth, which breeds fear and causes the deep inner wound to fester into a physical disease. Often the gift given to us in physical disease is missed because we are consumed with eliminating the physical symptoms.

Surviving the physical symptoms of a disease did not give me the same entitlement that comes with the process of healing. In the aftermath of cancer, I had no right to think I could help others with the same illness. There are no honorary healing titles awarded from surviving physical suffering.

While I was purchasing a smoothie from a shop close to my office, I spotted a woman whose bald head was wrapped in a scarf. I recognized the distinguished emblem of chemo and felt an instant kinship with her; after all, we both had a membership in the same club. It was not a club most people revered. The few times I went without my wig, strangers' snide whispers about my baldness quickly proved that others didn't make the connection.

In addition to cancer, the woman in the smoothie shop and I had something else in common. It appeared she shared my passion for the nutritional drink as a way to add nutrients to her diet during a time when little else was appetizing.

I was in disguise, so she couldn't make the same connection that led me to our association. During the daytime, I wore a wig to show my allegiance with the walking healthy. A stone's throw from my office, where other hungry Realtors longed to find a weakness in their competitor, I was not about to reveal my secret life of cancer, but I felt an allegiance with the stranger and was eager to share with her what had helped me.

Because I assumed we were of like mind, with no introduction, I boldly extolled the virtues of a book written by a physician whose aim was to direct cancer patients past the physicality of their disease and to the mind-body connection. I spoke to her about a book I had not even come close to absorbing, past the intellectual stimulation a new outlook proposes. I could have just as easily been talking about a new song I heard that had a refreshing beat.

She said, "I read that book." Could it be we had another thing in common? Her tone changed as she continued to respond. With anger that was tangible, she said, "I think he is full of it! How dare he or anyone imply that I caused my cancer?"

Her response startled me the same as if she slapped me across the face. I had nothing more to say. I left the smoothie shop with a sense of sadness and the belief that cancer would steal that young woman's life. I felt disheartened by my failure to help. It hadn't dawned on me that I couldn't help. I hadn't figured out yet how to help myself. After all, I was the one in disguise. She may not have been ready to go beyond the physicality of her disease, but since I carried on like everything was normal, I denied the physical limitations the treatment for the disease demanded, which is one reason why I could not absorb the message cancer conveyed at that time.

I continued to work before, during, and right after my cancer treatments. If I felt lightheaded in front of a client, I would drop my pen so I could bow down to circulate blood to my head while I bent over to pick it up. If the client was so gracious as to beat me to picking up the pen, I suddenly had something in my shoe that required bending over to fix. A memorable close call at being caught with cancer was when I worked until evening with clients and picked them up less than twelve hours later to resume their house hunt. Horrified that my hair had begun to fall out that morning, I had to pick them up with half the hair on my head. Afraid they might notice the change in my hairstyle I was armed with a lie. My story was my friend came over last night to cut my hair since I am too busy to go into her shop. I always found a way to cover my cancer trail.

When the treatments were over, my deep-felt gratitude at a second chance at life served to propel me forward, but the path it projected me onto was the same. The year I had cancer, I was honored as a top Realtor in the state of Georgia, ranking number six in sales volume. I didn't linger on the subject of cancer long enough to reflect on what happened, much less take the time to incorporate any lasting change in my thinking. I used a crevasse—real estate—to escape the reality of cancer. I picked myself up, brushed myself off, and took my second chance at life. I used my exhilaration to fuel the status quo I was so terrified of losing. The only resounding difference was the idea that I could make a difference for others with cancer, despite my failed attempt in the smoothie shop. My next mission was to become a patient advocate. I decided to write a book to assist cancer patients in navigating the bureaucracy of the medical field. Fortunately, it was not the book I wrote.

Over enthusiasm can push the gas pedal to the floor and disperse in the wrong direction the energy we need for our own healing. The ideal I had about helping others, because I survived cancer, was a pedestal that fortunately got kicked out from under me. Where my crusade to help others began with the physicality of disease, it ended with me healing myself. "They that be whole need not a physician, but they that are sick." Matthew 9:12. The healer must heal herself by becoming whole.

My story began in 1996 on a day in May that seemed no different than most chaotic days in the life of a Realtor. I was consumed with multitasking among clients, my staff, sales contracts, and such. Although problem solving and calming people's frazzled nerves was part of the territory, the chaotic tide of normalcy abruptly changed directions with one phone call. It was the day I was told, "Ms Wellman, you have lymphoma." The results from a biopsy came back totally different from what I anticipated. I never felt so out of control of my life. My assistant and I were in the office together when I got the call. I hung up the phone numb. I spoke out loud, seemingly to her, but I was talking to myself. I said over and over like a mantra, "I am too young to die."

Cancer and its proposition of death definitely didn't fit in with the career success I was in the midst of living. Not by choice, I immediately became indoctrinated into the world of medicine. My experience was that the medical field had its own culture and language unfamiliar to the layman. As a cancer patient, I felt like I was dropped into a foreign country with a language barrier that made it nearly impossible to navigate the land, much less absorb the culture. My persistence to understand what was happening to my body was evident by the multitude of questions I asked. The answers were never given with enough attention to detail to satisfy me. It reminded me of when, as a child, I pushed my mother for the rationale behind a decision, and she said, "Because I said so." The supposed clarifying answers I received from my doctors and their staff were a familiar version of the empty reply my mother gave me. The only identifiable difference was the professionalism in which the medical professionals draped their answers.

It is said that energy follows thought. The way medicine is focused on the manifestation of disease, as a patient you are encouraged to do the same. As I waited for cancer to recur, I was making the recurrence probable. The type of cancer I had, according to my oncologist, wasn't detectable through blood tests, yet I had a regularly scheduled blood test every three months. Every time I was scheduled for a follow-up visit, I was full of anxiety, especially on the visits that marked the success check points, such as one year and three years. Five years was the big one. In between, any semblance of a symptom was an agonizing reminder that cancer may have sneaked back in. A minor physical abnormality set off a horrific wave of panic, more intense than my reaction to the original diagnosis, since I had a memory of the toll the treatments took on me.

Much like my mother, who lacked the resources to say anything more, when I pushed her to justify a decision she made, medical terminology erects a façade that serves as a protective shield. It protects doctors from facing their human frailty and protects patients from realizing the doctors aren't God. It was obvious from the outset that medicine compartmentalizes disease, limiting it to the physical body.

Whereas medicine compartmentalizes disease to the physical body, many alternative beliefs compartmentalize "the cure" to the exclusion of the physical level. Those healing modalities may be from the other side of the gorge, but they also omit the river that runs through the middle, connecting both sides. When both sides fail to admit they meet in the middle of the river, we are inundated with superstition that defends mediocrity rather than revealing the vibrant truth. Claims not grounded in physical logic obscure the whole picture as much as claims immersed in it. Without the totality of who we are, neither side can substantiate anything more than remission.

Some of the alternative theories reminded me of a beautiful flower cut from the stem and presented as though it grew beautiful without the messy dirt and tangled roots. The expectation that any level beyond the physical level is airy-fairy and should be exempt from the integrated whole belies the underlying order of existence. No level of existence is unimportant, unintelligent, or without order. Our energy must cycle from the innermost level of our Spirit to the outermost physical level and back. Unfortunately, it cannot find its way back if we have not carved out a path. Energy then circulates back to the highest level we have reached, which is usually the emotional level. It is way too much energy to be absorbed without throwing us out of emotional balance, and it ends up interfering with the autonomic system of the physical body.

Considering each person is made up of about fifty trillion cells, it is a miracle that each cell knows what to do and can simultaneously carry out its appropriate function without the person needing to be conscious of the cell or its function or that its function is carried out. For example, the liver performs the chemical functions of a power plant large enough to fit on 500 acres of land.

Consciousness infiltrates the physical body, allowing the body to be self-regulating through what we refer to as the autonomic system. Since consciousness reflects the spark of life often referred to as Spirit, the monad, or God, it makes sense that if disease occurs at the physical level, there is a distortion in consciousness.

It is impossible for the human body to operate solely by physical mechanics; such a belief contradicts the miracle of life. We confine our Spirit by the constraints of the unremarkable when we focus on what is reflected into the mundane physical level. When we do, we dam the flow of our Spirit's force. Until we conceive life based on a flow of energy, and not limited by the impoverished adaptation of physical form, we imprison the force of our Spirit, curtailing its ability to guide physical existence with ease.

Life-force is pure and unadulterated. The distortion that impinges an incorrect message on the autonomic system of the physical body occurs between our Spirit and the physical projection of consciousness. It is similar to a childish game called *telephone*, where one child whispers something into the ear of the child next to him and the same message follows around the circle until the last child blurts the message out loud. In my childhood, it was a favorite party game, because the final interpretation of the original message was always hysterical and much different from the original message. A distorted message is anything but funny when it occurs in consciousness, though. When life-force energy is funneled into a distorted pattern, disease is the result.

My search to integrate medicine with alternative healing led me to a compelling theory that put the onus on me. Where the medical doctors considered my cancer anomalous, there were newfound beliefs that insinuated I caused my disease. I was not ready to handle the magnitude of such an explanation. The closest I could come to taking responsibility was admitting I pushed my body too hard by working too much.

My recovery from the physical pain and fatigue of chemotherapy and radiation was quick, but an element of blame lingered. I let my body down. It is difficult to articulate the enormity of that disappointment. The guilt is comparable to how a parent feels when she makes a mistake that causes her child hardship. To take on full responsibility for cancer was more than I could accept when I was struggling with the fact that I physically overextended myself. I needed the added alibis of disease predisposition, being raised in a steel mill town, and the many such reasons that held me as a random victim of chance. Instead of jumping the hurdle that I alone caused my cancer, I attempted to climb over it, again and again.

Resistance is like a weighted cord that pulls us back to the starting line until we become strong enough to break free. What we resist, we need the most. Pushing against what we are afraid to consider brings the experiences we need to build strength so we can carry new truth

The reason car accidents are so horrific is that your body continues to travel at its former speed until it is stopped. The motion is usually curtailed by a windshield or dashboard. The danger of resistance is not the resistance, but the speed at which we move in the opposite direction, because sooner or later, the motion will be curtailed. If we are lucky, the speed at which we are moving away from truth is not too fast, and we can be stopped with a gentle disappointment. For me, those experiences were not benign.

The repercussion of my resistance was the worst medicine I was submitted to. The harsh experiences that followed were relentless. One day, though, as refreshing as a cool breeze in the midst of summer heat, it dawned on me that if I let cancer in, I could also keep it away. I felt empowered, not a result of piecing cancer together, but the result of piecing myself together. Once I reached the center point of despair, there was no way out but to go within. Confronting the core of my wound, not the latest medical breakthrough, enabled me to heal. Healing is ongoing because the depth of who we are is limitless. Each breakthrough, as it pertains to us, leads us to a deeper level of knowing ourselves.

Healing requires juggling responsibility with faith. The choice I made to embrace life in the face of death acted like a buoy in the water, lifting me. Where my desire to change was about being cancer free, I found that being responsible has less to do with outcomes than it does about knowing who we are. Learning about ourselves is like a match that bursts forth in a flame of courage that burns off fear, and what is left behind is the faith that we are being guided from within.

I am reminded of a computer program I use for video editing called Final Cut Pro. If the project browser cannot locate some formerly captured media, the browser indicates the problem. If it could speak, it would say, "I know it was here, but it is not here anymore. Do you want to try to find it?" It alerts the user with a big red slash across the name of the moved media file. My body, if it could talk, was doing the same. It was saying, "I know you used to be here, but you are not here anymore. Do you want to try to find yourself?" Instead of symbolizing the inner disconnect with a red slash, it used cancer.

A child might recognize the purpose of taking a bath, but at bath time still does anything possible to delay the task. We make a judgment each time we deny what is important to us. The judgment is the choice to make something else more important in that moment.

When we do not know ourselves, we are making a choice to project life-force energy through a distorted pattern rather than the pattern most compatible with who we are. A simplistic example is the woman with the propensity to express herself artistically, but since her parents overemphasized making money, and art is not normally a field synonymous with high-paying jobs, she chose business instead. Sadly, she has never felt at home in that world. She believes the long hours she puts into working wreak havoc on her health, but when she painted, time didn't matter.

Adopt a Highway

I attended a weekend workshop that focused on being in service to humanity. The instructor set out to teach the attendees how to incorporate into life the true meaning of altruism—the habit of taking action to aid others, with no expectation of reward. While the teacher meant for us to apply altruism in its literal form, I was reminded of the ineffectiveness of lasting change implemented from without.

Our first assignment was to provide a service to the community where we were staying. On Saturday afternoon, the other students in my group and I gathered to divide and conquer the trash on the main highway. The class was held in a small Texas town that had one main route to and from the Austin airport. We decided to leave our mark of goodwill by cleaning the miles of highway that stretched through the town where we were staying. Our effort that afternoon made us feel we were helpful, even when we were taunted by a car full of boys who threw litter out in front of us. After the class ended on Sunday afternoon, we headed for the airport to catch our flights back to our respective cities. As the car I was in reached the highway we cleaned the day before, I felt a sense of pride well up inside of me, because I knew I played a significant role in making it clean. I was crushed when instead I saw even more litter than had been there before we cleaned it. Filled with fast-food wrappers, beer cans, and wine bottles scattered about, the highway served as the Saturday evening party throughway. Our effort to clear the litter off the highway was not going to change the habits and patterns of the people who threw litter out their car windows when they drove by. Disappointment washed over me like a gush of water on a campfire. I could live with the wasted effort I put into the highway, but the incident became symbolically personal. I thought, "That highway is like my body, one day symptom free, but not necessarily cancer free tomorrow."

A respite from the physical symptoms is misleading. All remission really represents is a period where life-force funneled through an incorrect pattern gathers more strength against the imposed physical aids, such as chemotherapy and radiation. It is no surprise that recurring cancer is usually more ravaging than the original. Likewise, a vaccine may eradicate one virus but create a stronger strand of that virus in the future, sometimes so strong it is labeled a different disease. Some viruses have grown so resistant that almost nothing has been found to kill them.

Healing, unlike remission, is ongoing. The distorted patterns that cause disease accumulate over years, and sometimes lifetimes, before disease manifests. We can't expect to make a change overnight in the patterns that no longer serve our wellbeing. In extreme, we may think that death is the end of our suffering from disease, but physical death, as the end of one lifetime, is not the end of the distorted patterns we failed to break before we left.

The weaker the tension around the distortion, the less resistance has accrued, causing the potentiality of disease to become only a probability, labeled perhaps as a predisposition in the next lifetime. It can also become a major malady, when the resistance accumulated over lifetimes turns into armor encrusting any other resolution to break the distorted pattern. Each new incarnation contends with the same obstruction to wholeness where we left off. The new incarnation starts with more vitality. Just as a good night's sleep provides us with a fresh outlook on our problems, each incarnation is ripe with potential to break through resistance that has imprisoned our expression. The continuity of life tidies up what doesn't otherwise make sense; for example, where disease is experienced, but not seemingly deserved, or deserved but not experienced.

It is considered a medical mystery when someone pushes past the pessimism written throughout her medical chart and heals. A physician friend said, "I learned to deal with a patient who died under my care by realizing that life and death are beyond medicine. There is no other way to explain one person's death, when medically he or she should have lived, and the person who survived, defying medical reasoning. As a physician, I learned we are a facilitator of life and death; we don't cure anyone."

The mystery is resolved if you can conclude that more is in motion than surgery, medicine, or early diagnosis. The flow of life is from the inside out, and on the inside is where we heal, not inside our physical body, but in the consciousness that permeates the body. Otherwise our energy rejects the distorted patterns it is funneled through, the same way a transplant patient may reject a kidney that is not a match.

The memory of cancer is not all encompassing, nor is its effect the lightning bolt flashing to brighten a dark sky. It is a reminder that healing is an endless inner journey. I once thought of cancer as darkness trying to take my life, but now I see it is a shadow that is there to obstruct the light. The shadow of cancer is a constant reminder that life is not meant to be all light, nor is it meant to be all dark. In the balance I heal.

WHAT WE DON'T KNOW
WILL HURT US

One night I came home exhausted from a hectic day. As I locked the door behind me, I felt relieved to be home. If someone gave me the winning numbers for the evening lotto, I would have hesitated to venture back out to buy a ticket. Not five minutes later, my sister called. I heard the strain in her voice as she said my name. In an instant, I knew something was wrong. Her dogs got into a fight, and she thought one was badly hurt. Being tired no longer registered in my mind or body. With a sudden surplus of energy, I got to her home in record time. When I arrived, blood was everywhere. It looked as though I had entered a murder scene. Still reeling from what happened, she didn't notice that she was the one badly hurt. We spent the rest of the night in the emergency room, where her finger was attended to and she received antibiotics, a tetanus shot, and a lecture from the doctor. The gist of it was that it is not wise to stick your hand between fighting dogs. He used the word *stupid*.

The speed at which I arrived at my sister's house and the precision at which I assessed the situation that evening was automatic, without hesitation or thought. When I reflect on that night, it is as though I am recalling a movie and not a memory from an event I participated in. It was not my conscious mind that mobilized or coordinated my actions; I was under the influence of fight-or-flight.

Our fight-or-flight response allows us to perform amazing feats, like the hero who saves a child by lifting the car she is pinned under, the soldier who holds his fellow officer in his arms, along with his severed limbs, or the EMT who removes someone from a car in the knick of time before the car explodes. The human transforms into a super hero under the adrenaline rush of fight-or-flight.

Animals in the wild display prowess and stamina that appears incomprehensible to humans. Inherent in us is the same proficiency, though. Animal nature is the basis of mankind. The courage, strength, and accuracy we demonstrate during a fight-or-flight reaction are proof. Our animal nature, impressed by unconscious recollection, enables us to respond to an emergency with power and finesse that surprises even the physically adept, in hindsight. Under fight-or-flight, both physiology and consciousness narrow their focus, allowing the intensity of our response to expand and fully meet the specific need at hand. Human beings then demonstrate what normally is unprecedented in their daily routine.

Once upon a time mankind literally had to fight or run for life. Civilization has evolved beyond constant, physical assault. The obstacles that threaten our survival have diminished, since we are no longer at physical risk every waking moment. We can go to the grocery store to get food and not have to worry about whether we will survive the hunt for dinner.

The upgrade in our external environment has not been mimicked by the interior of our mind, though. The unconscious mind has remained fixated on the physical concept of time and space that aligns with the conscious mind's existence for a single lifetime. Any shift in our world threatens the cozy den of beliefs our unconscious has nested in, and we experience the shift with the same intensity as the threat of death. Adhering to the concepts we are comfortable with, because our unconscious is terrified of change, keeps our life stuck in a repetitive pattern. Since life is dynamic, it demands movement and the constant changes that coincide. Because the unconscious mind is able to detect what our conscious mind cannot concretize, many times we are impressed from the unconscious level by a pending shift in our world. The result is generalized anxiety that keeps us in fight-or-flight mode.

For example, in a relationship, I am sensitive to any shift in my partner, which leaves me on high alert, rather than living in the present moment. My pattern around loss was inflamed by my childhood, beginning with my father's leaving and my mother's preoccupation with financially supporting my sisters and me.

In general, with intimate relationships, the people involved have to distance themselves before they can move closer. Emotional intimacy is about sharing our feelings with another, but begins when we become aware of our innermost feelings, as we learn about ourselves in relationship to the world and others. The process can't be done well with outer interference. If my partner is going within and I am terrified of the distance, I am likely to ask for reassurance, but because I am not conscious of that unconscious impulse, it does not always come across as harmless. Asking is not the issue, but how I ask can be antagonistic. For instance, after an argument, my partner may need to be angry at me before going inward and seeing where the magnitude of the anger blankets more than the recent fight. If I am trying to bring the relationship back in harmony because I fear distance, I may revitalize the fight just to reconnect, and the core of the issue is never seen as belonging anywhere other than in the relationship. Since the present moments build the future, the unconscious fixation on keeping life the same or stuck on the past as it relates to the present doesn't leave room for anything new.

Once reserved for physical survival, the same fight-or-flight re-action that protected our predecessors from danger coincides with every emotional reaction. The conscious mind mesmerized by the emotional drama is too preoccupied to break the cycle. Any impression from soul-level consciousness is taken hostage by the unconscious mind's fight-or-flight reaction. Before we can be receptive to higher awareness, we must relinquish all agendas. The single focus of fight-or-flight creates an impenetrable shield block-ing receptivity.

Physiologically our response is no different when we catch a spouse in an affair or cross paths with a bear in the woods. Like soldiers taking orders from their commanding officer, our cells respond to the "danger" message delivered by the unconscious. Our cells prepare for a head-on battle against the perceived, immediate threat, and their other duties become secondary. Primary responses under fight-or-flight do not permit the normal front-line defense against unhealthy bacteria or abnormal cells, such as cancer. We get scared to death over time, when our fight-or-flight response kicks in too often, and we cannot resist illness, as a result.

When we go into fight-or-flight mode, adrenaline gets flushed throughout the body and provides extra energy. If you are literally fighting or running for your life, the chemical reaction could save your life. If the adrenaline is produced in an emotional, stress-related reaction to a perceived but unreal threat, though, the toxins have no physical release. They take a toll on the body. Our energy is zapped, and our wellbeing is endangered when the body's autonomic system can't catch up from the missed cycles of immune defense, rest, and elimination of the chemical buildup.

While science acknowledges the physiological reaction and the impact on our immune system, it doesn't consider the contraction of consciousness and the impact on our actions. When the unconscious detects a threat, our nervous system, under the supervision of the unconscious, scans the environment looking for what needs to be defended against or avoided. Like a laser beam from a high-powered security system, our unconscious scrutinizes the environment and assesses the potential danger. Whether the threat comes from an external stimulus or an emotional stimulus, the response is the same. At the speed of light, the unconscious matches the stimuli to its database, like playing a game of charades, "It looks like..." The unconscious, as the past master, responds with a preprogrammed behavioral reaction learned when a similar stimulus was first encountered, perhaps even from another lifetime. Like peering through the sight on a rifle aimed at a target, the constriction of consciousness is an automatic survival defense that narrows the field of focus onto the perceived, imposed threat.

In the wild, survival means "kill or be killed." Driven by our animal nature, physical self-defense replicates the same primal instinct. If someone tried to take your life, in self-defense, you would attempt to kill that person first, and emotionally charged crimes of passion are no less animalistic. In the heat of an emotional reaction, a person can tip the scales past the point of return and savagely kill, as if defending physical life. Most of us would say we are far more civil than the people we watch on the news. Because we are civilized, emotional fight-or-flight may not be connected to murder, but it still propagates jealousy, competition, aggression, avarice, selfishness, and hate—all the personality traits that depreciate life.

At the end of each incarnation, the small portion of mind deemed the conscious mind is absorbed into the unconscious part of consciousness. With each new incarnation, a portion of the accumulated total is projected back into physical form as conscious mind for a new lifetime. With us from lifetime to lifetime, the unconscious part of consciousness is far more powerful than the smidgeon of conscious mind that exists for one lifetime.

The part of consciousness deemed the conscious mind is dense and therefore does not vibrate at the same frequency as the unconscious mind. For example, the unconscious part of the mind processes about 20,000,000 environmental stimuli per second, while the conscious mind processes only forty in the same second. If you apply these numbers to two armies, anyone could guess which has the advantage, more proof why positive thinking can be ineffective. Whenever our conscious intentions rub against unconscious fears, those fears awaken and sabotage our conscious goals. Blame is the deception of the conscious mind, as it believes the events that put the kibosh on those goals were out of our control. Likewise, seemingly benign issues become the spark that causes an emotional bomb to detonate before we realize the bomb is in our hands.

In the aftermath of emotionally overreacting to someone's comment, gesture, or action, we often can more easily forgive the other person than we can forgive ourselves. It is easy to conceive how we would do anything to fight for physical life, but much harder to comprehend an emotional reaction with the same fevered intensity. An emotional reaction is often followed by regret, once we realize our response had little to do with the present.

Even though the unconscious garners information from the past, the information can't be taken at face value, because we have added another element—the present. Keenly attuned to the present, the unconscious mind appoints its judgment about the present using data from the past. A gut feeling can seem like a reason to hesitate before entering into a business decision or entrusting someone we don't know. It can be an antenna, but the station has way too much static to trust the message. The unconscious mind is incapable of abstract thinking. Its limited view of the world is through our reactions to it.

Since I was almost eaten alive by a Rottweiler, I have a sense of fear around large, unleashed dogs. Unconsciously the thought is imbedded in my memory that without warning, such dogs attack. Multiplied by many lifetimes, we have infinite amounts of embedded recall that translate into warnings. The unconscious doesn't understand words, but interprets the environment by way of symbols. We program our unconscious with the thoughts, feelings, and actions that cascade into an emotional reaction. Every reaction imprints a pattern that becomes a habitual response to any experience that taunts an unconscious memory. For me, a large dog is an archetypical symbol that holds a lot of energy around fear. To someone else, a large dog is a beautiful pet.

Though not as powerful as the unconscious, the conscious mind has a broad spectrum advantage, because it can use the past, present, and estimated future. The conscious mind is not limited to the black-and-white reactions prompted from the unconscious. Since the conscious mind is more agile, it can detect shades of gray.

The conscious application of intellect, using diagnosis and discrimination, can offset an emotional stimulus and restore balance. This wedge-in of reason can broaden the limited, instinctual perspective of the unconscious. It is a pause between stimulus and response.

The interlude is not inaction, but detachment, where more information becomes available to determine the best action, whereas an emotional reaction uses all the energy to empower an action, often a wrong action.

Furious, a woman picked up the phone ready to blast her brother for the way he spoke to their mother. Her hands were shaking, he made her so angry. As she began to dial, someone rang the doorbell. The noise brought her back to the kitchen, in her home, which she loved. All of the sudden, the smell of dinner cooking in the Crock-Pot caught her attention. Dinner was going to be great that night; she hoped Roy liked the new recipe. Oh, yes, the door. Someone was at the door. On the way to the door, she was startled by how angry she had gotten with her brother. She wondered why she got so angry. She decided he was ungrateful. As a child their mother acquiesced to Steven's every whim, yet Steven was hard on their mother. The woman didn't understand it. Even as a child she never expected anything and worked for whatever she wanted. Her role as their mediator fit her strength, but was wearing thin after forty years of settling her mother's and brother's battles, especially now that her own life was so full. She met Roy a few months before, and the relationship was promising. She landed her dream job around the same time. The angst she felt around family issues robbed her of the happiness she deserved. As she opened the door to claim the UPS package the doorbell alerted her to, she realized she had changed, after all. Good thing the doorbell stopped her from dialing Steven's number. She didn't need to play her part in the play the three of them unconsciously contracted years earlier. The more she felt in charge of her own life, the less she needed to be in charge of anyone else's. She had to break the habit somehow.

The box she lifted from the door contained the new iPod she ordered. The Walkman she carried as she ran through the neighborhood was a dinosaur in the age of technology. Old habits die hard, she thought with a smile. The good news is old habits can be broken, once proven ineffective. It was time for her to leave her mother and Steven alone. Perhaps detaching herself from their relationship would force them to have one. She was grateful for the doorbell that gave her a chance to implement the old adage of "Count to ten before taking action." Even if it was by accident, it stopped her from making an angry call.

The conscious mind is like the geek with brains, but no brawn. It is no match in strength to the unconscious, which by comparison is the overpowering bully that easily coerces the conscious mind to follow. Those tenuous moments occur when our emotions are triggered. Rather than add reasoning to the mix, the conscious mind often becomes the tag line that supports the emotional reaction. A clue the unconscious has taken over are comments like "He made me so happy," or "Her incompetence made me furious." When we become our feelings, the conscious mind is along for the unconscious ride. We become hypnotized pawns, magnetically drawn to and identified by whatever incites our emotions. You would think we would stop when we feel the inevitable pain;

unfortunately, pain does not always break the trance. Sometimes it stokes the hypnotic fire.

It reminds me of the story of a man anesthetized for surgery. He was given enough anesthesia to put him in a trance, but not enough to take away the pain. He felt every incision, but from that trance state, he couldn't speak or make a gesture to alert the surgeon to stop the process that was causing him great discomfort.

This Message is Sponsored by Our Unconscious

The economic engines of our society roar from unconscious impulse. The advertising and marketing industry have used the power of the unconscious to its advantage. Since advertising has multiplied exponentially with the Internet, the advertising and marketing field can't rely on the consumer remembering a slogan. The days of recounting the crowning moment of an ad are long gone. From my childhood, Procter and Gamble's toilet tissue ad captured its audience with "Please don't squeeze the Charmin." Similarly, Wendy's hamburger ad got a lot of play out of "Where's the beef?" Now more than ever, successful advertising depends on bypassing conscious scrutiny and seducing our unconscious by reeling us in emotionally. The advertiser lends us an image in exchange for our money. Once our unconscious mind buys into the *feeling* the image sells, the conscious mind justifies the purchase.

For example, at least one credit card company sells its card, with its steep annual fee, on the illusion that carrying the card gives the cardholder prestige. Since I was a child, this credit card represented a symbol of prestige to me. It became my archetype for success. As an adult, I have to admire the brilliance in the way the credit card company markets its card. It offers the consumer a sense of honor to carry it. I gladly paid an outrageous annual fee for the privilege of carrying such a card.

A long-term cardholder with that major credit card company, I never missed a payment. Each month I even paid off the balance before the scheduled due date. As a result of my creditworthy history with the company, it offered me a second credit card. While credit card offers are nothing out of the ordinary, the bold lettering on the offer caught my attention. It said, "Interest free for one year!" A week after I activated the card, the company called to make sure the line of credit was sufficient for my needs. It was plenty. The only way the company could have been more accommodating was if it offered to make the monthly payment for me. It came close. No more than a nominal portion of the principal was required each month at a nominal percentage of the balance, and remember, no interest was charged on the balance for one full year. The timing was perfect. I was in the middle of building a home I hoped to sell before it was finished or soon after. My brilliant plan was to use the new credit card to pay for the materials, and when I sold the home, pay off the balance from the proceeds. Essentially, other than an insignificant monthly payment toward the balance, the materials wouldn't be a capital expense I had to pay for, nor would the debt accumulate interest. A proud platinum cardholder for eleven years, I certainly felt entitled to my flawless plan. Several months into the project, while I was making a materials purchase, that credit card was declined. Of course it had to be a mistake. I asked the clerk to please run my card again—and again. Apparently experienced at letting people down gently, she mustered up as much kindness as she could, apologized, and suggested I contact the credit card company.

I called, and my confusion turned into frustration, when over and over, I had to recount the series of events that led to the call. I was transferred from one department to another and even routed to a foreign country and back. No one had any authority to do more than follow a preset script that did not fit my situation. I was enraged over the wrongness of the situation, but my wrath over the episode transformed into an exercise in endurance. I spent nearly three hours on the phone trying to find someone who could remedy what I knew was a mistake. Finally I was vindicated. Someone at the credit card company discovered that when I made my payment the month before, an error occurred processing the payment, because I used a bank account different from the one I normally used. From my end, the phone-payment system took the payment and generated a confirmation number as proof. Unknown to me, the payment did not process as a credit against my balance. Once the problem was identified as a processing error, I felt relief. The ordeal was over.

Naturally I expected business as usual. Not the case. The company's computer system couldn't get past the status of a missed payment. The computer would not register the payment, even though it was the company's error. Since no human was willing to override the digital assessment of my creditworthiness, my credit limit got chopped down to the outstanding balance. I wish I could say that outside of the time I spoke to the credit card company, I never gave it any more thought. My anger was unshakable and spewed into my week like sewage from a broken sewage line.

About five days later, something happened on my construction site that demanded my attention. Once my focus on the credit card incident was broken, the monument of indignation I erected crumbled. When I reflected on the hours I spent that week calling, writing, and thinking about the inequity, regret took front stage, instead of anger. What I regretted was my waste of energy. The shift in attention allowed me to detach long enough to let go of the fight. Convinced I was fighting for justice, I could at last see my battle took on the intensity of fighting for my life. The incident triggered an emotional fight-or-flight response. I defended my worth, which I attached to a piece of plastic.

What Goes Up, Must Come Down

The level of consciousness that fuels our emotions is distinguished by attraction and repulsion from the unconscious versus compassion that provides a unifying balance from soul-level consciousness. Our degree of attachment or non-attachment is like the magnetic pull that influences a compass. Attachment and non-attachment point us to the physical world, binding us by the same cosmic law that defines manifestation—duality. On the other hand, detachment points our authority to a higher level of consciousness.

Duality is the steadfast law that governs the physical world. At the physical level, energy is reflected in its densest form. Each element of physical form is an aspect of the whole and not a totality unto itself. Like a hologram, the whole is present in all the parts, and the parts make up the whole. Similarly, the ice cubes made from a quart of water are parts of the whole quart. While the same volume and essential nature of the water is in each cube, the solidified form separates the original quart of water into pieces of the whole. Since we can't eliminate duality, at best we can understand it. By understanding it, we can eliminate fear.

Fear is the result of the illusion that by clinging to one side or repelling the other side of duality, we have captured what we want or escaped what we don't want. What we capture is only a gradation of the whole, in which the other half is contained.

Fear binds consciousness to an emotional loop of fight-or-flight. There is no way to integrate life from a fear state of survival, fighting or running from the one half of wholeness. By now I hope you see the connection. The emotional level supports duality. In a state of emotional motion, we are not receptive to inner knowing, but protect our position of duality, until the cycle is broken. Sometimes we are lucky and something jars us out of the fight-or-flight cycle or we jar ourselves as we build on the ability to detach. My mother was not so lucky.

My mother spent her life in survival, alternating between fight and flight. Much of her life she reacted to her world, leaving few moments where she could take anything in for herself. The wisdom she gained from her experiences, she did not pass down to us, because she did not respect her own wisdom. If life didn't show up as she wanted it to, she didn't feel there was anything valuable to gain, and if there was an experience that gave her a desired outcome, it still meant little, because it wouldn't last. Because she indulged her animal nature, she had no ability to integrate life. To her, life was broken out between the haves and have-nots. She couldn't see how the haves sometimes didn't have anything, even if she was privy to their emotional hardship, some of which they would have traded every dime to avoid. It never registered that the have-nots were sometimes richer if you measured everything but financial wealth.

My mother is eighty years old, and her memory is failing her. I can't help wondering if the problem is the result of age or of her misuse of her incredible mind. If mind uses the brain, but we don't use the mind, does the lack of energy circulating to higher consciousness cut off the ability to use memory and the cognitive and reasoning skills that aren't in our brain?

They say with Alzheimer's, plaque forms in the brain, like the clogged arteries that block circulation to the heart. Sadly, I watch my mother's mind deteriorate. To others I exclaim, "What a horrible disease." To myself I reconcile her seemingly bad luck to living a life in survival mode. My mother had many gifts. The biggest was her pureness of heart. Anyone who met her felt that love. The closest adjective to define her big heart was sweetness. Even now with her condition, she doesn't leave the doctor's office without unsolicited hugs and kisses from the office staff. The heart center is not the emotional heart that instigates drama, but love in its purest form at the soul level of consciousness. Had she allowed herself the ability to integrate her life, she could have positively affected others in ways she couldn't have imagined. Unfortunately, she was too busy chasing down one half of the whole, terrified of the other half.

A detached perspective breaks the loop of fight-and-flight, as it forges a straightline, vertical assent in consciousness, where we are receptive to higher awareness. A vertical perspective is a view that contains the lateral dualities. For example, from the ground, I can see one side of my house at a time, whereas from an aerial perspective, I can see all sides. Seeing all sides is the perspective of compassion. One side of duality is no longer against the other, but the energy of each is merged together as a whole. Compassion comes from the wholeness blended from duality. There is not a still point of balance, but a subtle movement where grace and discrimination merge. It has little to do with us. It has little to do with another person. It is all about where everything connects. Getting to that place requires inner strength, because it is where we tolerate the discomfort of holding our fear without the distracting motion of fight-or-flight.

One of the greatest moments to practice detachment came to me two months before my best friend died. The reality of the possibility of losing him hit me as suddenly and severely as an earthquake, changing everything that made up my life. The drastic decline in his health made it clear the meter was running out on his life, and the prospect of losing him, the person I felt the closest to, terrified me. I always imagined that being forewarned about the death of a loved one would help ease the pain of loss. In my fantasy, time provided the chance to tidy up anything left unsaid, and the tearful goodbye would serve as a parting gift where cherished memories were recounted and the deep heartfelt connection validated. What I hadn't counted on in my fantasy was the part of consciousness, the unconscious, being wide awake and hosting a party for our individual fears. What was worse was that those individual fears collided. Rather than bringing us closer, they intruded on the closeness we shared, like an unwanted guest barging in during an intimate conversation.

I could not have cared more for the man. He had been my dearest friend for more than twenty years. He was the one person in my life who truly saw me, yet never judged what he saw. It was the closest I have ever come to experiencing unconditional love. The prospect of life without him was unfathomable, yet while he was dying, my ability to be compassionate was sparse. The expressions of my emotions were in reaction to my fear of losing him. The surge of energy from emotional fight-or-flight was a force too great. Exaggerated by that force of energy, my actions were equally as strong. I made it my responsibility to break apart my friend's illusion of recovery. Although my approach didn't provide him any comfort, my concern for his well-being was valid. If he didn't face death, he could suffer more by hanging on to physical life. My arguments were flawless but did nothing to convince him. When the fight became too much, I had to flee. Days went by, and I could not speak to him. I ignored his calls when the intensity of my fear was too great and I needed to disengage from the relationship. With either extreme, the fight-or-flight energy felt too strong to contain. In the rare moments when I could sit still with my fear, I felt a gush of sadness. Allowing myself to feel sorrow was like a pressure-relief valve that released the fight-or-flight energy. In a moment of balance, I could detach my grip on my fear around loss. The leap from fight-or-flight to detachment is often experienced by going to the extreme before containing the fight-or-flight energy. When we authentically are able to contain the energy, rather than discharging it into fight-or-flight, pushing us to an extreme, we meet compassion.

It reminds me of a story I heard about a man who was diagnosed as HIV positive. He said he was at peace with the disease. Immediately he forgave the person who infected him. Zen Buddhism taught him the outer jargon before he worked through the inner turmoil that usually followed such a diagnosis. Six months later, he fell in love, and his world exploded. Death in the backdrop of love made the threat of loss more pervasive in his life. The feelings he suppressed around being HIV positive, he could no longer contain. Until he not only faced, but also worked through his anger, all the pretty sayings and profound teachings didn't give him peace.

Each time I felt the feelings around losing my friend, something shifted. The spectrum where he and I individually gravitated finally blended. When I stopped forcing him to face his death, he stopped running from it. I was able to be with him and not do anything, which in turn comforted him. Since he no longer felt alone, his need to hide behind denial ceased, and he was able to wander into the waters of the unknown in my presence. That's when we openly spoke about death. I shared some of the stories from people I interviewed regarding death. He particularly was interested in the near-death experiences, when people touched the other side and came back to talk about it. He liked hearing about the peace and wonderment they experienced at their crucial time of death. He then openly voiced his fear of dying, and I let him know it was okay for him to leave. Suspended above the level of our fears, we left the world of duality and touched into oneness.

If the vibratory frequency of soul-level consciousness lifts us above dense, emotional reactions associated with emotional fight-or-flight, it is fair to gauge that an emotional reaction is not a directive from higher awareness. Guided by soul-level conscious-ness, we direct the expression of our emotions into selflessness. For example, my emotions expressed through compassion allowed me to capture people's stories about death for my movie, because the people felt comfortable enough to be vulnerable. They knew I had no other agenda. Compassion is the point suspended above the barrier of fear, where our actions are guided by inner knowing.

There is an ancient saying, "If you seize the lesser devil by the tail, he will lead you to his superior." Each emotional reaction has a trail back to what our unconscious determines is essential for survival. Often what we protect is not essential for physical survival, but an emotional attachment weighted with the same passion used to defend life over death. Inner questioning helps take us to the superior of the lesser devil, but not until we have broken the reactive state will we find significant answers. When we use each emotional reaction as a symbolic representation of where we are bound by attachment, we are handed an opportunity to open a previously clogged channel to reach higher awareness. We grow in consciousness by crumbling the myths that supported the superstitions that force meaning where meaning was not.

All four of my grandparents came to America from Greece by way of Ellis Island. I was brought up immersed in the traditions and customs of Greek culture, which is heavily sprinkled with superstitions. When I was a baby, an evil eye was pinned to my undershirt. The little blue glass eye was supposed to protect me from evil. Growing into childhood and becoming aware of my surroundings, I comprehended and believed the literal meaning I was told about the beloved evil eye pinned to my undershirt, and I kept one pinned to my pillowcase. As an adult, I realized it was only symbolic of protection over me, and in itself wasn't going to save me from anything. I discovered it was more important to lock my doors at night than to sleep with an evil eye. Now I wear an evil eye as a bracelet, not because I believe it wards off evil, but because it warms my heart to look at it, as it is symbolic of the care of a family that could not express love directly. In its indirect way, the evil eye said my family loved me dearly. We crumble a myth when we can see the meaning of symbolism rather than believing the symbol. That is how detachment works.

Once we experience detachment, an inner memory beckons us to experience it again. Anything that breaks the flow of a reaction without causing another reaction is in sync with detachment. In other words, eating into oblivion may be a way to detach from feeling pain from a disappointment, but it only feeds another reaction—being angry at yourself afterwards, feeling fat, and feeling bad. Exercise helps me break the energy flow from a reaction, even if it is a short walk. Writing is another outlet I use to break the flow of an emotional reaction. Sometimes I have to dispel the intensity of the energy before I can sit down to meditate. We each need to find our unique or similar method of counting to ten.

The Solution is the Problem

Detachment may be the solution, but for a while the solution can add to the problem. Paradoxically, even an assent in consciousness will provoke the perception of danger, since it shifts the boundaries of the cozy den the unconscious built.

I signed up for a weekly class on kabalah, a spiritual study program that required almost three years of dedication. Each week we began with a meditation that spoke to the unconscious through symbols. We were urged to do the meditations at home every day between classes. The class lecture was followed by reading the study material. We were encouraged to reread the material on our own and do the study guides at home. My class had thirty-two students. Only nine of us remained through graduation. Nothing was exciting about the class; it was devoid of emotional stimulation. Often I wondered why I went, since I never did any of the meditations or homework assignments, but something was happening. I experienced more periods of balance. Another clue was my ability to sleep through the night. I had become resigned to insomnia decades earlier, so sleeping through the night for me was nothing short of miraculous. Although I could never verbalize the nature of the class to friends who asked, they easily volunteered their description of the change they witnessed in me. They described it as peacefulness.

My results encouraged one friend to enroll in the next kabalah class. She missed the first week. She had a good excuse; she went to see a movie with a coworker. Mind you, it was a movie she had already seen.

The next week, she missed class again. Her excuse was something like her boss wouldn't let her off work. She is self-employed. As her excuses kept her from starting the class, I looked at my excuses for not fully participating. Initially I was convinced my reasons didn't seem as far-fetched as hers. Soon I realized my unconscious was actually more resistant to change than hers, since I had the results to justify a full commitment.

Our unconscious is very powerful. It can make our excuses seem real. The power it has over our lives is evident by our lives, not by the reasons we assign to justify life. If there is any disharmony in our life, the unconscious rules in that area. When our energy is directed from a higher level of consciousness, we attract what we need, not the cycle of tough experiences to show us what we don't need.

ONENESS CREATES SEPARATION

Lost in thought about nothing in particular, I walked down one street and up the next. The same route I walked less than twenty-four hours before became an uneventful backdrop, until something on the ground caught my attention. It was unmistakably clear that the brown mass was not part of the green, grassy area that colored the curb. Squeamish about creepy, crawly aspects of nature, I approached with caution. If it moved, my pace would have picked up in the other direction. Finally close enough, I was able to distinguish its identity. It was nothing but a feather. What stopped me from feeling foolish was that it was larger than any feather I had seen. Intrigued, I picked it up and held it in my hand to admire the markings closely. The blend of brown hues made the feather look like a product of a well-thought-out, manmade, artistic design. Its size allowed me to fathom how feathers were once upon a time used as writing instruments. My thoughts jumped to how as a writing instrument, feathers demanded a writing style that flowed—the advent of cursive writing. I practiced cursive writing in the air with my imaginary feather pen while my thoughts continued to drift. I wondered what type of bird produced the feather and whether birds shed feathers like animals shed fur. Content with my trivial curiosities, I didn't notice the serious turn my thoughts took until I was engrossed in thinking about the symbolic representation of the outermost features of nature. For instance, a leaf from a tree or a feather from a bird can determine more than the species it came from. The physical specimen can shed substantial information about the growth, sustenance, instinctual habits, and lifespan specific to that species. Compared to mankind, nature and animals adhere to cyclical patterns restricted by the parameters of their habitat and are easy to foretell.

When we think about an instinctual response, we normally relate it to animals, yet an instinctual response is detectable in vegetation too, although Mother Nature is more limited. At the most static end of the spectrum of life, minerals are often put in the category of inorganic, but they, too, are living substances that respond, be it ever more slowly, to their environment.

Minerals, plants, and animals are governed by a group oversoul, which is the body of consciousness for the force that propels their movement for the duration of their life on earth. They are graced by the impetus of God, though are not given the individual expression anointed to mankind, whereas mankind is adorned with an individualized expression and individualized soul to ennoble and strengthen adherence to that expression, or the spark of God within.

From the lowest to highest hierarchical order on planet Earth, whether mineral, plant, animal, or mankind, the physical facts correlate to the essence of the underlying force within each kingdom and validates the axiom, "As above, so below."

Our physical body, as the vehicle we use to imprint our expression onto manifestation, is a synthesis from the apex of the three lower kingdoms, mineral, plant, and animal. Our physical constitution incorporates the dense body of the mineral kingdom, the vital body of the plant kingdom, and the strong body from the animal kingdom. The awareness to realize ourselves in conjunction with self-will separates us from the lower kingdoms and allows us individualized expression surpassing the combined evolution of the three lower kingdoms.

People with pets may argue that their pets have their own will, but what is interpreted as will in animals is a habitual response to environment, better depicted as instinct. Mankind has the ability to refine instinct by pointing intellect to comprehending our Spirit. We stand erect on the next rung of the evolutionary ladder because we can reach up toward our Spirit while using the mineral, plant, and animal kingdoms as our foundation. Through self-consciousness, we embrace self-will. It is often referred to as *free will*, but the misconception is in the preface "free." We pay dearly when we make choices that oppose the expression of our Spirit. What seems like choice, however, is often choice relinquished and a reaction to the environment from the lower consciousness of our foundation. For instance, when we act as mineral man, we remain fixed, and any change is minimal, relative to a larger environment shift. As plant man, we take root wherever placed, subject to the ebb and flow of the surroundings as influenced by the cyclical patterns of life. While we indulge our animal nature, as animal man we are driven by an inner compulsion, but still in reaction to the outer world.

My late grandfather, Peter Palaiologos, was a good example of plant man. His brother, Nick, was the first in his family to arrive in the promise land from Greece. Eventually Nick settled in Ohio, where he called Youngstown home. He discovered a niche—an import grocery store—in this small, predominately ethnic, town. Shortly thereafter, he sent for my grandfather. It was never a question whether Peter would or wouldn't go. Once Nick was ready for Peter, he set sail across the vast blue sea, leaving behind the only world he knew, to work for his brother, and work for Nick he did, from the moment he stepped foot on American soil.

As soon as Peter was acclimated to his new environment and earning a living, it was time for the next cycle of his life. He was sent a wife from the village he left. She was not chosen because of any fondness he had for her, not even out of a preference he may have shared. She was next in line to be sent to the United States as part of a vast Greek network of arranged marriages.

My grandfather woke up the same time every morning and left before dawn to catch the first available bus. The same bus brought him home at dusk. The cycle that designated another day for him came to completion each night he returned, usually within minutes of the same time every night, unless the bus was delayed. After dinner he watched the same shows on television, with the exception of special network broadcasts. No matter how tired he was, he never went to bed before the nightly newscast, even though he slept through most of it.

During an era customary for merchants to close their doors on Sunday, once a week he had a day off, yet Sunday began no differently than any other day. Awake before sunrise, he faithfully abided by the parameters that provided his purpose for that day. The routine for Sunday was engraved in stone and based on preparing the family dinner. One step short of hunting, it began with defeathering a chicken that he then meticulously roasted with the potatoes he painstakingly peeled. Between the regular intervals of basting the chicken, he looked through the Sunday paper. Some fifty years after arriving in America, he still had never learned to read or write English. He translated the news by the pictures. The minimal English he spoke was just enough to enable him to function in the store. Hello, good-bye, thank you. Beyond those words, his brother Nick spoke for him.

His life consisted of whatever was demanded of him, but he demanded nothing for himself. His whole life—the country where he lived, the job he worked, the woman he married—were all dictated to him. He may have complained about his arthritis, walking from the bus stop in bad weather, or when his grandchildren asked him for a dime for ice cream, but he never complained about being in servitude to the demands of others.

An example of mineral man would be my grandmother's brother. He was the last living sibling on her side of the family and was still alive when my mother, sisters, and I took a trip to Greece in the early 1990s. We met our great uncle in the village where he was born, the village he never left.

He proudly showed off the dilapidated house where he and my grandmother, along with nine other siblings, were born and raised. If that house survived him, he would not have any reason to leave it. Since keeping track of his age served no usefulness, he had no idea how old he was and had to rely on what we pieced together as a good approximation. We calculated him to be in his early nineties, and though age reflected in his movements, he still manually tended to the same olive trees he gardened all his life, at first with his father, until old enough to work on his own.

Unable to think abstractly, he could not conceptualize beyond his world. A kind man restricted by minimal experiences, he knew little; his opinion of the world depended on relatives who ventured outside the village and returned. Since he lived by the sea, the bits and pieces he could interpret from the experience of others focused on their sojourn across the ocean. My mother spoke fluent Greek, and if she kept the topic enclosed by the circumference of his surroundings, she could elicit a response. Mostly he had no words to communicate what he felt, so he expressed himself through tears of joy at seeing a part of his surviving family he didn't know existed.

An extreme force is the only catalyst for the movement in mineral man and plant man. The outermost extreme can be the result of a freak act of nature that forces movement. For example, Hurricane Katrina forced the evacuation of an area, or as in the case with my grandfather, the response can be from the pressure of group guidance, be it family, a religious group, a culture, or society. The degree to which we abdicate self-will is the same degree to which we lack self-realization. A prerequisite to self-realization is awakening our strength, not as a stopping point, but to take the next step. Since animal man's self-realization is limited to how he compares and contrasts with his surroundings, it is still an external process and not the full disclosure of self-realization mankind is capable of achieving.

While animal man's strength is motivated by desire, in a group it can run the gamut from seeking acceptance to dominating the group. Animal man fights to maintain a particular position, but not necessarily the same rank within each group. For example, at work he can be seen as a ruthless competitor, yet the woman he is courting sees him as a loving, attentive man. The edicts animal man follows are internally prompted, but motivated by the sensate level of how he feels, while the stimuli that triggers that inner response is usually a reaction to the external world. Whatever means we use to seek an outer identity, our decisions are influenced by others validating the persona we identify with. The problem is that shallow identity acts as a surrogate for the enormous potential of our essence. In a weird way, it is like swallowing gasoline to power our car, because we are restricting our life-force to power the vehicle of our physical position rather than the essence of our expression.

For example, it was rumored that a pastor from a local church was released from his duties in the church because he was homosexual. A pastor does not have the necessary skills that can translate into gainful employment in the secular world, so he entered it with a minimum-wage job as a waiter in a local restaurant. Meanwhile, his wife fled the state with his only child, to be with her family in New York. Desperate to see his son, but with no extra money for a plane ticket, he asked a benefactor of the church for the money to buy the round-trip ticket from Atlanta to New York.

It is realistic to assume that when he was a pastor, part of his duties entailed making sure the financial donors were happy, especially those who contributed more. I imagine that over time a relationship was inevitable between him and those benefactors. While it is purely conjecture on my part, I suspect that relationship was proudly touted and periodically dropped into conversations as "The pastor is a dear friend."

The particular woman he approached was the heiress to her late husband's fortune. While she continued to uphold her late husband's generosity as one of the largest contributors of that church, she denied the former pastor the ticket he asked. Helping the homosexual ex-pastor was not in line with a behavior to which she attached her identity.

A different heiress to her late husband's fortune and another major contributor to the same church was eager to judge the woman who turned down the former pastor's plea for help, yet as the saying goes, "She did not put her money where her mouth was."

Worse than not seizing the moment as an opportunity to jump in and help the man, it became her chance to reinstate her image as being more generous than the first woman.

Within each of us the virtue and vice of mineral man, plant man, and animal man exist to greater or lesser degrees. A psychologist once told me, "Pain is mandatory; suffering is optional." As the adage implies, pain is an inevitable aspect of life, but the degree of our pain can be determined by the degree we allow these aspects of us to choose. Just as a ten-degree drop in temperature is more noticeable to someone sensitive to the cold, the greater our awareness is, the more sensitive we are to the pain from actions divergent from the essence of our nature. Only the man who is self-realized, as Joseph Campbell says, "answers the call." When we become self-conscious, our response to life is prompted from inner knowing, rather than a reaction to the outer world. Self-realization morphs the outer world, because rather than reacting to the external environment, the outer world becomes a symbolic reflection of the inner terrain and a means to know ourselves more deeply.

Not all growth has to be painstaking. Providence reciprocates when our choices coincide with the expressive energy of our Spirit. In those moments we find ourselves in the right place at the right time, which has a positive impact on our life. A transformational step becomes a walk as smooth and rewarding as that of a movie star's sashay down Hollywood's honorable red carpet. You can say the seemingly perfect external event was lucky, but luck is always earned. We reap the reward when our actions are a response prompted from within rather than from a reaction to outer pressure.

The film I am working on taught me a microscopic lesson, reinforcing the macrocosmic law about surrendering to the flow of life, rather than believing we can control it. Surrendering to the flow of life is an internal process where we are guided from an inner knowing rather than outer circumstances, and the outer circumstances are like the raft that moves us along the river. From the people I interviewed to the people I hired to support my work and all the steps in between, there is a knowing I have that as I do my part, if I surrender to the synchronicities, they flawlessly lead me to the next step, even though the process has been anything but flawless. The process has been laden with issues, as one can expect, but every issue proved to be a link to the next point of progression. For example, when I was ninety percent complete, I ran into technical issues and lost a co-editor, who had to take another job during the time lapse. Upset with the setback, by that time I was calmed with the expectation that something positive would come from it. Sure enough, in the gap of time working out the technical issues, I reconnected with the person I initially offered the position as co-editor. She had the time to assist me in finishing the project, whereas, at the onset she didn't.

What hinders us is the implicit structure that is impressed upon us from the collective unconscious. It pushes us back down the evolutionary ladder where we respond to life as mineral, plant, or animal man. The group mentality has become absorbed within our personal unconscious. No doubt we were stalwart supporters in past incarnations, because of the hold it has on us today. Our loyalty is reminiscent of the semblance of safety it once provided. Survival characterized mankind's adjustment to physical living. Safety was collectively determined by outcomes. If the red berries killed someone, the precedent was set, "Stay away from the red berries." There was power in numbers when we were developing the skills to adapt physically, and the group protected itself by providing those numbers. Now mankind is accustomed to physical existence and has rendered that need obsolete. As Gandhi said, "Strength of numbers is the delight of the timid. The valiant in spirit glory in fighting alone." The functionally obsolete pattern of adherence to the group mentality stifles our unique expression and encumbers us by precepts such as "supposed to be" and "should be." A dependence on group mentality limits our rise in consciousness. Likewise, rebelling against it keeps us held at the same level of survival as abiding by it does. The other side of the same coin is duality, and we never rise above the coin toss.

The sign said "Honk if you are for peace." Many cars did. I drove by in silence. As I approached the last of the protesters, he looked me in the eye and gave me the finger. Apparently he was not happy with my lack of support otherwise noted by a loud noise, which was anything but peaceful. The only way we have an impact on the world with peace is by remaining detached, despite the battles we are surrounded by, personal and collectively.

Our potential is found above the level of duality. We tap into that level when the result is not the reason for doing. Otherwise we circle our expression with the hungry sharks of fear, doubt, and insecurity. "Am I doing this right?" "What will he think?" Endless chatter usurps our energy until we are so heavily weighted that we tumble back down the evolutionary ladder. For example, if someone was in the car with me, I would have probably honked. It doesn't seem so threatening out of context, but in the bigger picture, that is exactly how we fan the flame of outer pressure while ignoring the inner fire of our individual expression. We get so caught up following a norm, we fail to see the ineffectiveness of it. Worse yet, we fail to see how it keeps us ineffective.

A new paradigm calls for us to think outside the box. Simple as it sounds, it is not simple, because we have to step outside the box before we can think outside of it. My friend teases me when I tell her I am doing a construction project. She says, "If you are not physically doing the work, you are having it done." My preference is acting as a contractor, not the subcontractor I hire and oversee. Since I am not hands on, but am around construction work, it is actually easier for me to conceive of a different way to get something done, which comes in handy when there is a problem. I am not limited to "This is the way its done," since I am outside that box.

As pioneers of a new consciousness, we can no longer pay homage to an old structure. The herd mentality is unable to use life-force to promote higher awareness. Since we don't need the strength of numbers to adapt physically, we must untie the ropes that hold us bound to a group consciousness, because they disable our abilities. The trick is detaching at the same time we embrace the fact that we are part of the whole.

The oneness from which we began purposefully created separation, because each of us has a separate, unique expression to put into creation. The expression we are assigned is abstract, but permanent, whereas what we create in the physical world, though definable through our senses, is temporary. The essence from the experience, in harmony with our expression, empowers the whole. The way we handle the experiences we encounter, and not what we physically create, has the potential to raise the vibration of the total. When we are not ourselves, we depreciate divinity, or the whole. Similarly, cancer cells, which follow a distortion of the intended pattern for the type of cells they are, take energy from the physical body.

I listened to a friend vent her anger about how we outsource all our labor to less expensive foreign markets. While she was going on and on, naming companies that were guilty, I knew we are all guilty. We squelch our expression not only from the mandates of an outer world, but also from our lack of discovering our inner world. A lot of times we outsource self-responsibility because we don't take the time to know who we are. Only when we take the time to know who we are can we be receptive to inner knowing. Otherwise we use the consciousness of mineral, plant, and animal man, rather than using the strength of the lower natures to strive higher in consciousness.

A young man around twenty-five years old goes to Mozart and asks him for advice on writing symphonies. Mozart suggests to him that he is too young to write symphonies. The young man gets confused and reminds Mozart that Mozart himself had been writing symphonies since he was ten years old. Mozart responds, "Yes, but I wasn't asking anyone for advice."

If we all try to be the same piece, the whole no longer reflects oneness, but one.

NOTHING OCCURS
WITHOUT DIVINE INTENT

Be sober, be vigilant; because your adversary the devil, as a roaring lion, walketh about, seeking whom he may devour: Whom resist steadfast in the faith, knowing that the same afflictions are experienced by your brethren that are in the world.

—Peter 5:8-9

Punishment was the staple of my childhood. Usually I was grounded, losing the privilege I enjoyed most, my freedom. Even in the face of adversity, though, my appetite for mischief never ceased. The risk of punishment apparently was worth the reward of fun, or more accurately, I gave little thought to the possibility of being caught. My will overrode any menacing consequence, even when the consequences intensified. What started out as being grounded from going outside after school one day easily escalated into being grounded from all extracurricular activities for the month. I never blamed myself for the repercussions from my actions. My mother got the bum rap as the bad guy. I took refuge in the comfort that each passing year meant I was one year closer to becoming an adult. With every birthday, my excitement escalated around the anticipation of life as a grown-up. Certainly it didn't include punishment. My childish perception of adult life meant I could do what I wanted, because I wasn't going to punish myself, was I?

A man I interviewed for my documentary on death barely survived a horrible car accident at the high cost of not being able to function the same way he did prior to the accident. Right after the accident, he wished he was dead, because he was left a paraplegic. Before the accident he lived on the fringe of life, drinking, using drugs, not doing anything purposeful, while destroying himself and those around him in the process. Now he is an inspiration to others. Because he has climbed back from the point of deep despair, people call him for advice when they lose hope. The way he described the moment he realized he would never walk resembles the way a mountain climber describes the moment he is aware the rocks underneath his footing are giving way, right before he falls. The difference between the two is the mountain climber is launched into the depths of physical pain, but the man I interviewed descended into excruciating emotional pain. We spoke several years after the accident, right before he began motivational speaking. Through his experience he is not only able to encourage others out of their pit of despair, but he can also inspire them to make better choices. Did he have to have the accident to reach the place where his life was in sync with his divine expression? Possibly. His Spirit may not have been able to get him past his will without such a severe consequence. He insinuated he may have ignored the kinder, gentler, knocks that attempted to get his attention.

Free will is like the choice to lift one leg in the air while standing on the ground. The other leg, the one we can't lift, keeps us standing and represents the larger force that we don't control, but it seems to have the final say over our life. Try lifting both legs at the same time. Regardless of how badly we want to, we can't. What is this greater force that keeps us grounded to this life, yet is nearly impossible to define in earthly terms?

In Dostoevsky's book *The Brothers Karamazov,* one of the characters said, "I am trying to find out where your God is, just to return to him the entrance ticket, the entrance ticket to life. I don't want to be here. And if there is a God, he must be violent and cruel, because without asking me, he has thrown me into life. It has never been my choice. Why am I alive without my choosing it?"

It sounds absurd to say we chose pain. As adults it seems we act similar to the way I did as a child when I was oblivious to my part in the infraction that led to my punishment. Whether or not we are aware, we always choose. The gentleman from the accident, in a perverse way, chose his fate. Since the greater will of our existence remains unconscious to us, we can't always understand choice. We differentiate free will as the will of mankind, while the greater force is often defined as God's will. The fallacy is that God's will is the will of some omnipresent being separate from us.

If we come into life with a secret mission, free will is our ability as mankind to make the choices needed to fulfill our mission. Since learning is not a straight line, often the wrong choices bring us closer through the awareness we gain before we cycle to the next level of energy. The greater will of our Spirit provides the path of energy, and we choose the genre of experiences most compatible to it through a growing awareness of ourselves. In the words of Ernest Holmes, "Humanity is divinity wearing a mask." Learning who we are is the process of peeling away that mask.

Prayers to God, the universe, Spirit, and such fall on deaf ears, because only through human hands and human feet can we manifest our expression. When we apply ourselves to life through experiences incompatible with our Spirit energy, though, we create an imbalance that seeks balance. Life is a series of experiences of reaching balance through imbalance, although we falsely label the imbalance as mistakes. The greater force, energy of our Spirit—analogous to the leg we can't lift—creates a magnetic pull that draws to us the circumstances and situations that need to occur for us to be brought back in alignment with our greater will. The great mystic and teacher Helena Roerich repeatedly said, "Blessed be thy obstacles."

Macy adopted her daughter Devon when Devon was four. By the time Devon was in first grade, her teacher expressed concern to Macy about her daughter's inability to make friends. It wasn't from a lack of effort on Devon's part. She tried, but lacked even the liberal social graces allotted to a six-year-old. Macy became defensive and assured the teacher nothing was wrong with Devon other than the natural adjustments for a child being placed in a new environment. Each year, during parent-teacher conferences, Macy defended the same concern. Not until Devon was in eighth grade did she finally find a friend—a thirty-four-year-old neighbor who lived three blocks away. Macy came home from work several hours after Devon got off the school bus. She believed Devon when Devon told her she had spent those hours doing homework and watching television. Macy didn't see Devon's fingers crossed behind her back when she told her mother what she did each day after school. Devon was so happy to have a friend who loved her that she had no problem keeping the secret they shared. He assured her it was common for friends to have secrets the rest of the world wouldn't understand. Macy was no longer able to turn away from her daughter's problems when Devon was four months pregnant.

We are always being told something through life. Nothing is an accident. If we observe what is put before us through someone's words, through our experiences, or through an interaction, we are being fed an implicit message. The inner tension caused when we go against the energy of our Spirit is similar to the tension of two weather patterns that eventually converge, causing a horrific storm. If it weren't for the technical indicators that alert the weather stations, we wouldn't have much warning before the storm hits.

In life, we have indicators when our will opposes the will of our Spirit. Usually we are defensive and hold a particular stance or position against any outer interference, but rather than bringing harmony to our life, our stance adds chaos and pain. The illusion that we are in control overrides being able to register that the heat has been turned up on the chaos and pain. Similarly, a chef once told me, if you cook frogs, you can't immerse them in a pot of boiling water, because their natural reaction would be to jump out. You have to slowly add heat to the pot, making the change in temperature too slight for them to notice.

Out of chaos comes order, and usually order occurs when our resistance to change is forced by an outer event too drastic for us to ignore. The breaking point often is referred to as *reaching bottom*.

Devon's issues were not separate from Macy's. Macy had to face her own issues of neglect through Devon. While it appeared she wasn't present for Devon, outside of the immediate survival needs of her daughter, Macy was less present for herself. She spent a lifetime avoiding her own pain. She too was molested by someone she trusted, her father, but buried the memory. Her daughter had to dig up the memory and lay the remains in front of Macy, before Macy would look at the skeletons in her past. Being a mother to her daughter was an intense process, littered with landmines filled with regret, guilt, and shame.

Talk Radio

Recently I heard a woman on talk radio extol the virtue of balance. She alleged, "If you eat a balanced diet, work and play in balance, and sleep the correct hours of a day, your life will reflect balance, and you will attain peace." Unfortunately, those descriptions are derivatives of balance. Inner balance is a labyrinth of conflicted intent. Our Spirit and soul-level consciousness are opposed by our unconscious and conscious mind, and more often than not, the levels of being become harmonized by way of painful, disharmonious, counterbalancing experiences. The paradox: balance is often restored by non-balance.

The yin and yang of life is an inner collision of opposition that is made apparent outwardly. We don't reach a synthesis of balance outwardly until the momentum within recedes. The components of balance feel like anything but balance being restored. The tension from the inner collision sets up the vortex of energy that brings us the experiences we need, to find harmony, even though the experiences seem unbearable. Oddly, the degree to which we are capable of becoming out of balance reflects the power of our Spirit to the same degree.

We can learn by experience or we can learn through awareness. Awareness doesn't take away all pain and suffering, but it transmutes the energy that is feeding pain and suffering into uncovering who we are. For example, in the midst of an argument, I can focus on my part of it, looking at why I reacted to another's words, or I can feel hurt and angry by what was said, making it personal to me, when it was a projection of the person who spoke harshly. Awareness minimizes the propensity to learn through the exhausting process of the same argument, where we believe the right words can make the other person understand something different. When we obsess over a problem or react emotionally, life energy is added to the chaos. Conditioned to participate in the movement, we rarely rise above it while we are immersed in it, which is why we give up on rituals that help us detach. The ritual is often an extreme to the way we live, and therefore its immediate impact as a balancing movement is not felt, and instead more chaos is experienced around the inner conflict.

Back when I worked incessantly, I decided to meditate as a means of relief, thinking it would add peace to balance out my otherwise high-stress career. I bought the right music, the right candles, and the most fragrant incense and marked off an hour of quiet in my Day-Timer. As the words were telling me to let go of all my cares, I was reminded of all my pending problems. No matter how serene I made the environment, I could not stop the inner chaos. My mind was a whirlpool of thoughts about my day, the next day, and my "to do" list. I felt like a failure at meditation and shortly thereafter blew out the candle, snuffed out the incense, shut off the music, and gave way to thinking. The irony is the only way I could run away from the chaos in my mind was to stay busy. When I focused inward and shut out the outer noise, sitting still was like being tied to a track, hearing the train. I grew more frightened, the louder it got. What I didn't know at the time was the train eventually passed on the adjoining track.

Life continually moves, which means a living balance is never absolute. Keeping a living balance is analogous to moving from room to room with a cup of tea, when it laps from one side to the other but doesn't spill. Anytime we can watch the movement of life the same way we look down on that cup of tea, we have risen above the movement. Our higher self is the judge, but from that view there is no judgment. Good isn't considered better than evil; both just are. Both are a form for the force of life and are necessary to maintain a living balance.

Did God Make a Mistake?

My sister and I were in a fight when she said to me, "You are not infallible; only God is." With that comment she personified all that is right and good with God and all that is wrong and evil with humanity, which is the belief we have been taught. No one bothers to explain how all that is wrong and evil occurs under God's authority. When our prayers don't seem to be heard, or when disaster strikes, does it mean God made a mistake?

On the inverse, it is not a gift from a benevolent God when we are in sync with the flow of our Spirit. The paradox is that divinity does not instigate cause and effect. Life-force just is. When it is said that "Nothing occurs without divine intent," it means there is an immutable law of balance, and existence is under the jurisdiction of that law. Balance is the divine intent that nothing occurs without, and it reconciles both good and evil. A quote from the ancient fable *The Hitopadesha* sums it up well.

> Even whilst moving in the solitude of the sky,
>
> The birds meet with disaster;
>
> Even from an unfathomable ocean,
>
> The fish are caught by the skilled ones;
>
> So in this world,
>
> What indeed is an evil or a good act?

God is not outside of us. God is the life-force pervasive in multi-dimensions and exists through multi forms, from subatomic matter to human beings. As mankind, we are one of the forms in one of those dimensions. Our force essence coalesces and is inseparable from divine principles. Our Spirit embodies the pureness of these principles of divinity in balance. As the principles of divinity are expressed through consciousness, they are opposed by our resistance to growth. Resistance or unawareness can be called *evil* when it manifests as authority—the authority of a leader, to the authority of a parent. Evil is an opinion meant to overpower people from thinking for themselves. At the dense physical level, the principles of divinity are manifested through duality, where each principle has a virtue and vice. The paradox is that it is from resistance or unawareness that we grow.

The other day while I was riding my bike fast, the idea hit me that resistance is part of the movement forward. As the road resisted my tires, it gave me something to push against to cause my motion. Some resistance is good, but resistance crystallizes when it is supported. When we support resistance, comfort is vying with growth for control over our lives. For instance, when I ride my bike, I feel a breeze against my body and that feeling compensates for the pain of peddling a long distance. Over time if resistance becomes stronger than the forward motion it instigates, we become stuck. If I reached the base of a mountain, the mammoth form would stop my movement forward. Likewise, when we feed unawareness through our application of the vices of the principles of divinity, we stop growing. What keeps us stuck is a component of comfort resistance maintains, which feels better than the discomfort change introduces.

Every cycle of energy accommodates a higher frequency than the one before, to stimulate our ability to learn the virtue of each principle. When the energy is not used in accord with its potential, rather than supporting life, the energy supports resistance. For example, when truth ceases to be uncovered, honesty, as it is used to develop the principle of divinity—truth—turns into criticism, as resistance to truth. Sadly, the critical person has the same capacity to seek truth, but misapplies that virtue into a vice.

I remember when a priest in my school told me, "You will burn in hell!" I was in high school grappling with finding myself and renouncing God, as I did any authority over me. The priest was reprimanding me for hanging *Playgirl* photos of nude men all over the halls. It was yet another rebellious act on my part, and since no one saw me doing it, the nuns and priests of the school relied on me to confess. Of course, confessing was the last thing I was going to do. I stood my ground while the religious leaders scrambled around to get me to submit by threatening me. I didn't budge. I already figured if there was a hell, I was going to be in it one day. From that day forward, I was branded as junk. In their failed attempt to teach me honesty, they criticized me over and over. They met their mountain, a child with a will stronger than their ability to be honest with themselves. I broke the moral code they had idealized as right and wrong. What was wrong is they stopped being true to themselves.

Rather than using their religion as a means to expose inner truth, they used it as a weapon to disparage another.

Knowledge founded without experience is like oil on top of water and does not become integrated. As e.e. cummings said, "Knowledge is a polite word for dead but not buried." We can study the ancient texts that incorporate the essence of the divine principles, but because those principles are the life within us, they can unfold only through experiences that make them personal.

On the journey of life, self-development is layered. Although each layer uncovered itself may not seem significant, the accumulated synthesis is significant. Similarly, each step on our assent is by itself not meaningful, but the accumulated steps take us to another level. While truth may have always been important to me in theory, I had to learn through experience what it really meant. For instance, I was taught not to lie, but it didn't stop me from lying. When I got caught skipping high school, I became more careful not to be caught the next time. With my first real job out of college, I lied to my boss. Had he not liked me so much, I could have gotten fired. The possibility of losing my job made the stakes higher. Unemployment was a consequence I clearly did not want. Although more reluctant to lie thereafter, I still hadn't integrated what I learned about the importance of truth. My perspective of lying slightly shifted, but only to eliminate the potential consequences of being caught.

Next I was lied to by someone significant and experienced the other side of a lie. For a while I was too caught up in my emotional pain to integrate that experience as my advocate for truth. Once the emotions dissipated, I was able to use that memorable encounter to overcome my temptation to lie. Eventually truth became my natural, inner compulsion, regardless of whether lying provided an escape from conflict.

The layers of integrating a principle are endless. Now I grapple with the areas in life where I lie to myself by justifying actions that don't make the grade on the standard of ethics I hold everyone else accountable to.

Truth is a principle of divinity that I empower each time I exercise truth over a lie. Empowering the principles of divinity is similar to weightlifting. With weightlifting, it takes time to build muscle strength, but it takes less time for muscles to atrophy in the absence of weightlifting. Muscle weakness is more noticeable after a week off from weightlifting than the strength gained from years of dedication.

Just like we are meant to exercise our muscles, we are meant to exercise the principles of divinity, which is why there is no grand reward for doing it, as opposed to the noticeable inverse degree of consequences when we fail to focus on inner development.

Each divine principle is an aspect of truth. As that principle grows stronger inside of me, I am more empowered to bring forth my expression in life. As Soren Kierkegaard said, "Life has its own hidden forces which you can discover by living." Everyone has the same potential to expand awareness by developing these principles of divinity: diagnosis and discrimination, intellect and motivation, individuality, devotion to our inner being, courage, adaptation, realization of our inner self, love, understanding, and wisdom. The development of an inner principle doesn't indicate right use, just as a high IQ doesn't guarantee good grades. A higher awareness is not synonymous with intelligence, but usually indicates a greater empowerment through inner principles developed over lifetimes. The temptation to use higher awareness to enact the vice rather than the virtue of divine principles also becomes stronger as we become more aware.

The difference between higher and lower awareness is the impact. One such person with a high awareness who enacted the vices of the principles of divinity was responsible for millions of people losing their lives. His name was Hitler. A fact that most people don't know about Hitler is he had Max Muller translate the ancient wisdom teachings from Sanskrit, and Hitler then enacted the vice of those virtues to gain control over millions.

On the other side of the globe there was a primitive man who could discern weather patterns with better accuracy than modern technology, just by observing the constellations in the night sky. His predictions aided his small tribe in timely preparation of shelter and seasonal harvesting. While he enacted the virtue of diagnosis and discrimination, his impact was relatively isolated.

Divine principles are neither harmonious nor disharmonious, but the quality, as the form we express them through, is the cause of harmony or disharmony in life. The way we express love is a prime example. If it is through jealousy and possessiveness, other areas of our life will mimic the same self-serving expression. The epitome of creation is when divine principles are expressed through the attributes of their most compatible form. You have heard me say it: we experience harmony in life when we are in line with the expression of our Spirit. Our expression, as we apply it to life, like life, is not static, and develops and changes with the movement of life over time. We can look back on each phase of life as the stair steps that take us from one level of awareness to the next.

My experience in real estate had less to do with what I accomplished in the outer world than with what I developed on an inner level. The inner strength I developed from that career was invaluable and paved the way for me to express myself through another form, where I would reach another plane of inner development. We reach a plateau of growth after we have exhausted inner learning through one phase of life. If we don't change directions with the flow of life, we will be forced to do so by what seems to be outer circumstances. It's comparable to walking down a path and continuing straight, into the middle of rough terrain, even if the road veers right. For me the rough terrain was a series of catastrophic events. While my losses appeared to be with the outer world, the real loss was a connection to my inner self. Soren Kierkegaard said "The biggest danger, that of losing oneself, can pass off in the world as quietly as if it were nothing; every other loss, an arm, a leg, five dollars, a wife, etc., is bound to be noticed."

With each layer of development, we strengthen the characteristics that bring more of our expression into manifestation. For example, patience is a characteristic that enables the containment of power. It procures the ripe moment, whereas, impatience short circuits receptivity in favor of wanting what we want when we want it, be it fame, fortune, recognition, a relationship, or something else. When we are impatient, we use power to express divinity through the negative quality, pride. Patience allows us to act out the positive quality, or virtue, to the vice of pride. Patience is having the awareness that our inner being is guiding us. Such devotion relinquishes control and empowers individuality.

We seem to think that each decision we make is a choice between one outcome and another, which is a myth. The decisions where we wrestle with our intellect or emotions will have the same end result, the same lesson needed to be learned. Actions guided by intellect and emotions alone are karmic, where some principle of divinity needs to be further developed.

I have heard people say, "If only I didn't do such and such," as if the lesson they needed could have been avoided otherwise. If we are off our path, the form we choose for our expression will be similar, regardless of whether the experience looks dissimilar. For example, when someone's identity is attached to success, his or her attachment will reflect as egotism, no matter what job or situation the person chooses. Not to worry; the lesson we need to learn will be delivered, no matter what. There is no perfect choice. Sometimes we postpone a decision out of fear of making a mistake. Indecision is a choice in slow motion and does nothing to avoid what is inevitable. Depending on the cycle of energy, the lesson may be more intensified, the longer we wait. "Blessed be thy obstacles."

When I interviewed an anesthesiologist for my documentary on death, I asked him, "In the process of anesthetizing a patient, were you ever afraid you would accidentally kill a patient, either by administering too large a dose or being unable to reverse an allergic reaction from a proper dose?"

He answered, "When I first began, I was afraid, but after a close call, I realized fear negatively impacted my work, so I worked hard to overcome my hesitation. In the proceeding years, I went to the other extreme and became cocky, but after another close call, I realized overconfidence also negatively impacted my work. Somewhere between respecting the process and assurance in my abilities was the balance I worked to maintain, but oddly I couldn't hold that balance until I learned more about myself."

At one extreme he was waylaid by insecurity, and at the other, overconfidence. Fear and overconfidence are opposing sides of the same coin—egotism, often expressed as pride. Insecurity may appear different, but it is the same. Both are too much focus on a false expectation of what we should be, rather than being in alignment with who we are. The duality of the physical experience allowed him to know both sides of the coin. First through his insecurity, and then through overconfidence, he created the close call that touched on the possibility of another's death. Balance shows no mercy. While he pulled at the fringe of tragedy, fortunately he didn't need to experience it full blown, before he learned. He shared more about his journey and the details along the way. The outcome was a man getting to know himself.

"If you desire to be good, begin by believing you are wicked."
–Epictetus.

A common self-deception is believing we are not like a parent, because we act from the other side of a negative quality they represent. Rebelling against what we didn't like is not much different from the anesthesiologist who went from fearful to cocky. The other side of the same coin is still an act against us and not the development of us. Whether we admit it or not, we wouldn't have incarnated with the parents we had, if we did not have the same undeveloped qualities. It's like a reversible jacket, where either side, although it may be a different color or fabric, is the same jacket. By acting out the duality of our parents' shortcomings, we carry forward the sins of our lineage.

I spent my childhood watching my mother exhibit phenomenal strength, even though she didn't internalize that strength to build her self-confidence. By divorcing my father, she broke the chain of female oppression customary in my Greek culture and deeply rooted in our family's lineage, and she did many years before divorce was common in our modern culture. Since a young girl, I was my mother's cheerleader, and I continued to encourage my mother throughout her life. I said things like, "Look how strong you are! You raised three daughters with minimal help from Dad!" When she felt stupid because she didn't advance with technology and learn to use the computer, I said, "Are you kidding me? How were you the number-one sales clerk of a ritzy women's boutique, if you are stupid?"

I grew up vowing to myself that I would not be the same as she was. I was not going to go through life timidly. Like the swimmer who pushes herself off the wall of the swimming pool to gain momentum in the opposite direction, I pushed off my mother and walked boldly through life. Was I really any different, though? I tried so desperately to be different that in the process, I compromised my expression the same as she did. My issues looked different, because they were the other side of the same undeveloped qualities and in a different generation, but where she appeared insecure, I appeared overconfident. Both of us were encapsulated by our own concepts of who we were, and therefore we bypassed developing into who we could be.

It is not enough to speak in terms of love and light. The development of the principles of divinity is submerged into our everyday experience, as we teeter between enacting the virtues and vices. Fortunately God's law—balance—never allows the inner light to burn all the way out.

AFTER THE FIRST DEATH, THERE IS NO OTHER

On my fiftieth birthday, like all forty-nine birthdays before, I blew out my candles while making a wish. Less than thirty days from my birthday, I got that wish, followed by a torturous three weeks of self-torment, deciding whether or not I wanted what I wished for. If I had foresight, I would have forgone making a wish before blowing out my birthday candles.

The wish itself is as insignificant as telling you what I ate for dinner. The emotional crisis I experienced had nothing to do with getting my wish, even if on the surface it seemed as though it was the cause, because deciding whether or not I actually wanted my granted wish consumed me and became the focal point of my life to the exclusion of a normal life. On any given hour, my granted wish added pep to my step and became something I looked forward to, until it flipped into the last thing I wanted. The churning of my mind was almost audible as I abruptly went from being consumed by logic against the wish until logic was overruled with my desire to have the wish. On the surface, as it often does, it appeared that my battle was between intellect and emotion, so I listened to both with the intense focus of a juror trying to attribute guilt or innocence to a defendant. Even when I was sure of a verdict, the closing argument of emotions swayed me in the other direction. There was never any conclusion, because even my emotions switched and contradicted their initial plea. Before I knew it, my emotions were against the wish, and logic was for it. Both sides had two opinions, and there was no telling which opinion would surface or when. The only sure thing was that each side opposed the other. No matter which direction I momentarily accepted, life fell into place to support it. I couldn't even rely on outer clues, because they were as fickle as my mind. It was as if four people were inside my head and each was capable of rallying support or opposition. I was in a loop of insanity that had nothing to do with the wish, and it made a mockery of my intellect and emotions.

Having my mind in overdrive caused tension throughout my body, and I felt every molecule of serotonin deplete from my brain. While all this indecision and stress was happening, a part of me watched, amazed. That part was like the judge pounding down his gavel with a distinct, resounding "no." Without feeling or a reason, it ruled against my wish.

The chaos of my chattering mind was not as resolute. In a deranged way, my inner battle became an expression of control, as I operated under the illusion that I had authority to decide yes or no. On the surface, nothing seemed out of control, but my unconscious mind was consumed by fear, because it sensed death. It was no coincidence that during the same period, my best friend's life was coming to a close. His dying process stimulated my internal war, adding a log onto an already roaring fire, but his pending death was not the cause of my inner battle any more than my wish was. Although his dying was not the catalyst, it surely was a reflection of what was occurring for me internally. On an inner level, a part of me was dying. Another layer between the outer world and my inner world was shedding. All the while, the charade between intellect and desire was a distraction from my fear around that inner shift. All stops were pulled out to be noisier than the resolute observing part of my being, which was attempting to gain dominion over the noise I used to deflect it.

During my interviews with people about physical death, I found it is a common reaction in those who are physically dying to become ambivalent. They flip back and forth about what they want and don't. It is as if they, too, feel their ability to choose leaves them a vestige of control, while the ultimate death looms overhead. On an inner level, they can hear the countdown of their remaining breaths of physical life, but the volley of physical life is the diversion they place between life and their fear of death. Something insignificant as what time the next meal is served can be a decision fueled with the same nonsensical urgency I experienced around my granted birthday wish.

Death is not reserved for physical death, defined as the moment life-force disconnects from the physical body. We are given plenty of opportunities for a dress rehearsal, in any sudden shift in life as we know it—a breakup, job loss, financial deterioration, illness, or a belief shattered. Whenever life-force disconnects and unties the knot that binds us energetically to something familiar, even if done willingly, fear snakes through the unconscious. Positive events illicit the same response, such as breaking a bad habit, getting married, buying a home, losing weight, or winning the lottery. Although they aren't associated with loss, they initiate change, where something familiar is given up in the exchange. The unconscious is at the level of the animal nature and can keenly detect any shift, similar to the way a dog senses someone is about to knock on the door before the sound penetrates our awareness. Since what the unconscious detects is not a tangible death, it makes no sense to our conscious mind, but the fear that registers in our unconscious can be as strong as the fear experienced while facing physical death, our own or a loved ones. Consciously we try to reconcile that fear to something in the outer world, which has nothing to do with the inner shift, such as my birthday wish. An inner shift hollows out an uncomfortable void in the psyche. The psyche then tries to return us to our prior state, restarting the bad habit, regaining our lost weight, or frittering away a relationship or financial gain.

The inability to surrender to that void encourages us to cling to impermanence, like clinging to the vapor of an exhale on a winter day, mistaking it for the breath that keeps us alive. Our energy is focused on what is slipping away. We force a tighter grip on the past and disregard our future to silence the hypnotic melody in our mind that goes something like, "should have, could have, would have." Too ensconced with the inner chatter, we don't notice that the sacrifice of the past holds the power of the future. Stuck in the delusion that what silences the noise in our mind is a movement toward feeling better, we miss the fact that our energy is spiraling in the same place, similar to car tires spinning in the mud.

The inner battle is a smoke screen. Purposefully, the part of our being that is eternal is orchestrating change. It is the mustard seed that has the power to move the mountain. Foolishly we believe we can stop the momentum, but the only thing we prolong is our pain.

Laurence Gonzales writes in his book, *Deep Survival*, "For most people it's unthinkable to imagine what appears to be a solid mountain coming apart. But all mountains are in a state of continuous collapse. The disconnect between that reality and our perception leads to many accidents." Maybe it is our perception that we are in a solid state that surprises us when an inner shift occurs. If, like a mountain, we are in a state of continuous collapse, it is no wonder that we fervently fill any void with life in an effort to shore up the inevitable collapse. Since we fill that void with what is dying, we add to the decay already present, culminating in the inevitable collapse of an unforeseen, critical event.

Until we reach the point where we realize a relationship is not going to save us, money is not going to save us, and obtaining something more is not going to save us, we keep piling weight onto an already weighted system of outdated beliefs, as we frantically search for something to save us from emptiness. For example, some dying individuals extend their physical lives through medical care and prolong their physical suffering with no quality of life to warrant it. The departed, difficult relationship becomes attractive, draped in the fantasy that it miraculously will be different this time. The alcoholic thinks drinking in controlled amounts won't be a problem. The magician of desire makes us see the flame that once burned our hand has become a flower waiting to be picked.

If we understood death is never absolute and the debris from the decomposition of old forms clamber together to create the foundation for the next step, we wouldn't need the necessary crisis as the gateway where we are forced to leave old structures behind. The gestation period of rebirth is not apparent to our physical senses, which is our nemesis. Mystically the period is called "the dark night of the soul." Before daylight, the height of temptation converges with the peak of intolerable, and our reaction is to rummage through the graveyard of the past, pulling out a corpse and believing the illusion as it veils itself in new life.

Death is part of the cycle of life, from the literal physical death making way for rebirth through reincarnation to the changing beliefs that lead to a rebirth in how we live. There are countless deaths and rebirths every day, all the way to our breath, which mimics the cycle of death and rebirth. The exhale forces the death of one breath to allow for the rebirth, or inhale, of the next. Like the life-sustaining cycle of breathing, the cycle of death and rebirth are the sustenance of life.

When we limit ourselves to the duality of the physical level, we see death as the opposite of life and betray the necessary process in between. Grief nurtures the gestation period before rebirth. If we fully allow grief, eventually we reach acceptance and understanding. Acceptance is the final push before new truth is free to take form. In that state of sorrow, we become receptive to understanding life as it is, rather than keeping the delusion of how we think it should be. Fledging truth is fragile and can be easily lost, if it is not consciously integrated into life through action. Our journey is predicated on how we navigate grief. Everyone reaches crossroads and makes choices to turn inward toward understanding or reach outward toward distraction. There is no correct turn, but life defined by our journey is an inescapable, infinite cycle of death and rebirth.

The way we deal with physical death is symbolic of how we deal with change. People I interviewed who faced physical death said they really believed they would avoid it. Intellectually they may have said, "One day I will die," but when they were forced to face their physical death, they were surprised they couldn't sidestep it. We are surrounded by death, but we doubt our death will occur. Consciously we live each day as though death is a remote country we'll never reach, yet unconsciously we fear it at every turn. The reverberation from that fear seeps out as the motivation behind most of our actions. We attempt to bury fear in the busyness of life, and then we wonder why life has little meaning. Our meaningless busyness is spiritual laziness, because it lacks an inner connection.

Non-acceptance of death is the root of fear, and that fear is the architect of our suffering. Because the tentacles of suffering are so intertwined with life, they choke out life's meaning. The meaning to life is embedded in death and not in the busyness we use to avoid it. Until we accept death as part of life, our suffering holds no purpose. When we accept death, the purpose of suffering is revealed.

Elizabeth Kubler-Ross created a model for grief through her research of people dying. In summary, she concluded people go through stages, which she labeled as denial, anger, bargaining, and depression, before reaching the final stage of acceptance. Denial— "This is not happening to me." Anger—"Who is to blame?" Bargaining—"I'll do anything for..." Depression—"What's the point?" She was brilliant and courageous as a pioneer, paving the way through uncharted territory.

Although her research concluded that the stages of the grief process do not necessarily follow a specific order, I believe it is incalculable to force grief into stages, like a stage of growth that morphs into the next stage; for example, baby, toddler, adolescent, adult, geriatric. While making my documentary on death, I did not find the common thread I set out to discover. Instead, those dying and the people they left behind experienced grief as a colorful tapestry that gave meaning to life. The surface did not reflect the complex, individualized process that went into creating the design.

When the intensity of emotions is too great, we block them before they have a chance to weave understanding into our life, from where a whole picture is revealed over time. We pause behind denial, anger, bargaining, or depression when the intensity becomes overwhelming. Unfortunately, the reprieve becomes comfortable, in contrast to the intensity of emotions. Avoidance pulls at the threads of our life tapestry. The longer we escape grief, the more the meaning of life escapes us.

One person I interviewed said, "Grief is a beast; it can sneak up on you at any time." Rather than categorizing grief into stages, I found it cyclical. It is loaded with potential as it spirals full of meaning and depth when we face it, or it circles the periphery, hiding behind impermanence when we run away from it. Using the behaviors Elizabeth Kubler-Ross labeled as stages, we live the cycle of grief, coming closer or going further from the meaning loss is meant to impart. The behaviors she refers to as stages, I consider a smaller cycle within the larger grief cycle, full of potential aware-ness, where we pause and integrate meaning, provided we don't linger too long. With that in mind, denial is the distraction instigat-ed through transference of desire, such as work, sex, drugs, alcohol, and overeating. Those things make us feel good or give us gratifica-tion. Anger is the irritation we attract to keep us occupied. Bargain-ing comes in different versions, "As soon as I____, I will be happy." Depression is the hopelessness we feel when denial, anger, and bargaining don't work, and we are forced to face our grief, but we are usually more receptive by then. Depression is full of potential. If we can ride its waves of powerlessness, it will bring us to the shore of acceptance. There are cycles within cycles, and the duration varies. Every time we hit acceptance, it doubles back and works through the unfinished grief of the past. As Dylan Thomas said in one of his poems, "After the first death, there is no other."

I had a love relationship that ended seven months before my dog was killed by a car. Not until I was grieving the death of my dog was I able to accept the ending of that love relationship and assimilate the meaning from that loss. The grief we avoid from many death and rebirth cycles in life becomes backlogged. The accumulation is like a giant mound of snow, waiting to be melted from the tears of sorrow. We are given the opportunity to touch back into that depth of sorrow from intense life experiences that captivate our attention. They are a net that falls down around us, holding us still, to grieve.

The death of a loved one forces us to deal with grief. People I interviewed for my documentary on death spoke of their time grieving the loss of a loved one as a rare epoch, when the world stopped and nothing else mattered. People reach a core of sorrow during that time that is so penetrating that it transcends everyday life and takes precedence over every other aspect of living. Despite all that is known, possessed, or desired, regardless of dreams and hopes, nothing but grief is significant at that time, and nothing in the outer world can fill the inner void. A mother who lost her child described it as "A big gaping hole that nothing can fill."

A friend and I were reminiscing about our mutual friend who recently died, and my friend expressed what I had thought many times. "If only I had another chance to see Barry, there would be so much more I would ask him about himself, so much more I would share." He wasn't expressing regret over something he left unsaid or undone or something he had done wrong. Instead, the finiteness of Barry's death left the space in my other friend's life to take in more life. I had been thinking the same thing for a while, but hearing him voice what I didn't understand allowed me to piece it together. I realized we both were experiencing the side effect of grief. Because of the nature of emotional intensity around death, nothing on the outside can lend comfort, which is why it is common to integrate life around death. In a quirky kind of way, integrating life is like catching up. The blend of conscious, unconscious, and soul-level consciousness is powerful, like the tailwind pushing a jet. We can't help being pushed forward into a blank space that gives us room to contain more life, which is how we plug into our power. Since Barry's death was the catalyst, we naturally focused our desire to fill that space with more of Barry's life.

Sometimes no specific catastrophic cause, such as death, makes us circle back and reach a depth of sorrow. We just run out of energy and can no longer escape accumulated grief. Denial, anger, or bargaining demand more energy than we have left, and we can no longer keep the door closed to our mound of suppressed grief. I see that situation with my aging mother. Once a vibrant woman, she no longer has the energy to outrun sorrow, which is closing in on her remaining life. At nearly eighty years old, she battles depression. After consulting with her doctor, I found it interesting to hear that the antidepressants don't maintain the same barrier between the individual and depression with the elderly as they do in younger people. The elderly must frequently change their antidepressants to stay one step ahead of sorrow. I suspect the vitality of youth aids in the fight, the way a young person has more strength to fight off viruses and germs.

Whenever sorrow is triggered, part of the frozen mound of grief we avoided melts. Sorrow is receptivity to new life, but with sorrow, we are saying goodbye to something old. If we resist the temptation to fill the space, we will be guided to what we need to experience next. While we are each being led, our life's mission is revealed. A purpose implies an end, but there is no end. Like truth, our purpose evolves. Life is infinity broken down by each cycle of birth and death. Our purpose, like truth, is not absolute, but evolves as we do.

Claire's Story

Claire is a woman I interviewed for my documentary on death. Success driven, she set out to conquer the business she was in and continued to do so long after she loathed every minute. She used her energy to fill an outdated form not even remotely compatible with who she was. Prior warnings triggered her to reevaluate her life and pay attention to the inner shift, but she was too occupied with filling the consequential void with a life she conditioned herself to follow. In Claire's case, she had to die, literally, to be reborn into a new awareness.

After a car accident, she was pronounced dead. Her parents made the trip to the hospital expecting to identify the body of the daughter they loved. To their joyful surprise, Claire came back to life. Before long, her parents realized that in her near-death experience, the Claire they knew had died. Awakening, she met their tear-filled eyes with a strange request. The first thing she said was, "Bring me some paint, a brush, and canvas."

Her father said, "But Claire, you don't paint."

She responded, "I do now."

MONTEZUMA'S REVENGE

In school we had to write a report about the historic leaders we studied, although I never understood why, since history books recounted the lives of these people for us. I suspected we had to write a report to show we were paying attention. My report about Montezuma might have read something like this: The documented history that reveals Montezuma's character portrays him as an exceptional leader, specifically noting the positive changes he implemented during his reign. Unlike his predecessor, he was genuinely concerned about the wellbeing of the Aztec people he led. The decisions he made were based on their needs and not on personal gain. Not only was he a revered leader, but he was also a formidable warrior. History credits him with leading his army into forty-three victorious battles, making it apparent he was passionate about extending his authority. The vast territory he accumulated and controlled in the early 1500s is known today as Mexico and Central America.

If I were to write that recap of history today, the outline would be driven by my curiosity. His decline is more noteworthy than his reign. Entrusting another with the role of god was his downfall. My curiosity would linger on his unrelenting need to give his power away. The tragic collapse of his dictatorship probably had nothing to do with his leadership skills or strength as a warrior. He projected his belief in the presence of an outer god onto Cortez, who was the man that fit Montezuma's image and likeness of a god. Since Montezuma was convinced Cortez had more power than he, he bowed under Cortez's authority.

There is a time when all of mankind is presented the chance to visit the land of the fool's paradise laden with illusion. The length of our stay or frequency of our visits determines the extent of our demise. It is fair to speculate that Montezuma met his downfall as a result of overextending that visit.

The fates of these two men collided when Cortez arrived at Montezuma's territory with his unskilled army of one thousand trailing behind. No one would have viewed their critical meeting as a threat to Montezuma. Any observer probably would have judged Cortez's brazen behavior as stupid and consequentially fatal. Montezuma was backed by an experienced army, and insulated by the sheer number of people under his reign. His capital city alone had 300,000. Although the power of an army is usually determined by a combination of experience and allies, between these men, it turned out that neither mattered. Montezuma surrendered his power to Cortez by acting out his belief that Cortez held the power that Montezuma lacked. Montezuma imprisoned himself by an illusion he saw as truth, but the illusion formed his prison cell.

If I had to pinpoint the moment of his defeat, it was when he defended Cortez's truth rather than his own. Energetically, it was then that Montezuma stepped down from being a powerful ruler. When Montezuma handed over his inner authority to Cortez, the masses lost respect for Montezuma. Within a year, the people revolted, Montezuma was killed, and chaos and corruption fell on the empire.

Like all tales, there are variations in the story of what happened between Montezuma and Cortez, but we don't need details to grasp the meaning. The lessons in history, when uncovered through hindsight, are usually compared with all the seemingly smart choices we've made. Human error, once discovered, seems to elevate us above the same deficiency, which is a mistake. It is more accurate to assume any human behavior is alive within us all, even if it lies dormant until triggered.

An illusion is like a free radical in the psyche. It causes an imbalance as it erodes inner strength. Every time we assign our power to something we believe to be more powerful, we hold a part of ourselves captive. Outer idolization is often defined as infatuation, a Latin derivative meaning "made foolish." The foolishness is rooted in the irony, since we are seeing our power projected onto another, reflected back at us, but we interpret it as belonging to the other. When we see our power as belonging to the other, we view that person with awe.

We have an example of Montezuma, a powerful man who must have considered the cause and effect of his decisions, since he had made so many good choices as a leader and warrior, but he handed over his power to a less competent man. Are we afraid of our own power? Do we fail to realize how powerful we are? As with any challenging multiple-choice question, if the list of possible answers includes "All of the above" and "None of the above," I would be stuck deciding between "All of the above" and "None of the above."

How powerful we believe we are is subjective. A belief, like trust, is weighted by the significance to our life, and that weight of importance can shift at any time. For example, our belief in the meteorologist's accuracy holds less weight than our belief in the pilot of the plane we are boarding, but more weight to a couple getting married in an outdoor ceremony. Power becomes weighted as important when we feel we have none and not so important when we know we are powerful.

We usually feel powerless during periods when we are over-whelmed and our ability to cope becomes stretched beyond our capacity to reason. The feeling is like being dropped into a body of water. Submerged in powerlessness, we fear we are going under. The catalyst is usually an occurrence that obstructed the direction we thought we were headed. The relationship we thought was ours forever has ended; we failed to make partner in the law firm; we lost our home in foreclosure; a family member is ill; a person we held in high esteem has disappointed us; and so on. Part of the illusion in fool's paradise is that any one person, place, or experience can give us power, providing a boost above the discomfort of life. In fool's paradise, we subscribe to eternal happiness. Facing that our dream has been stymied, even if we were unaware we were chasing one, leaves us with the feeling that the subscription has run out. What we have chained ourselves to for power all of the sudden is a weak link. Tension builds each time we are let down, and the breaking point makes us aware that what we held onto for power was not power at all. The weak link never provided a solid connection to inner power. The weak link was only an illusion used to compensate for the lack of inner connection. The compensatory fill-in, be it success, recognition, religion, a guru, or relationships, eventually ceases to hold, and we are left with a feeling of separation so potent that it is experienced physically, as if we could drown in our despair. The feeling of disconnectedness makes us believe something major is missing, not as if we misplaced car keys, but as if part of our gut has been ripped away, making us think life is unbearable. What we chained ourselves onto for power gave our life meaning, but meaning is once again out of reach.

Children today are far too smart to be outwitted. When I learned to ride a bike, at least a month passed before I noticed the training wheels were ever so slightly lifted, and I was riding on my own. Recently I observed a bright six-year-old learning to ride her bike. Every time the training wheels were moved, she noticed and refused to ride until they were planted back on solid ground. Regardless of her ability to ride on her own, she believed the training wheels were the reason she could. We act no differently when we maintain a belief that power comes through something outside ourselves.

Psychology has labeled abandonment as the primal wound that arouses a high level of anguish. Abandonment is a diagnosis of a childhood wound caused from an early experience of feeling separated from our primary caregivers, physically or emotionally, before we had the capacity to reason. Since we had no ability to survive on our own, the preverbal interpretation was that we would die. The shock of that trauma becomes unforgettable. Any succeeding experience that rubs against that initial wound causes intense emotional pain.

Most of my life I was told I had abandonment issues because my emotional reactions to separation often were out of proportion. Any loss would throw me into emotional turmoil. Nothing outside of me relieved my pain, and as tenacious as I am, I tried everything. I didn't know how to deal with the intensity of the pain I felt. Being given a reason for it did little to change my anxiety around separation. Many years later, I arrived at the conclusion that abandonment was not about the absence of nurture in childhood. My childhood abandonment was a reflection of lifetimes of accumulated behavior antagonistic to my soul. The central ache was from the loss of connection to my innermost self, and any outer occurrence served as a reminder of the powerlessness I felt, being disconnected from my power source. I suspect this lifetime is where I have reconnected, but the pain is cumulative. Any perceived loss rubs against a deep, longstanding wound, giving me another avenue to solidify a connection and stop abandoning myself.

If you poll the masses about the least helpful things people can say when we are in the depths of despair, "We are never given more than we can handle" would be ranked at the top. Those words never provide comfort. We want our problems handled, and we want to be out of pain. Rather than complete the cycle of pain, where the understanding of our soul is there to console us, we reach for the mirage of a comfy cushion we can rest upon, such as the belief someone or something can give us what we need. The longer we reach for what feels good, the greater the abyss that separates us from connecting to soul-level consciousness. To see outside in the dark night, we have to dim the interior light. Each time we seek outer comfort from inner pain, we have dimmed the guiding light of soul-level consciousness. When we perceive life through our physical senses and interpret it through our conscious and unconscious will, our conclusions are left to the emotionally charged assumptions from the logic and response of our senses. We conform to fit these distorted truths. Since they aren't based on inner truth from soul-level consciousness, we are constantly conned by an illusion, yet we count the change we get from a purchase to make sure we weren't cheated out of a dime.

Every morning I am reminded of how easily we become focused on the illusion that something outside of us can give our life meaning. I try to sneak in a few minutes of solitude with a cup of tea before the demands of the day greedily snatch my time. Recently I have been joined by my new puppy, who is content in my lap, after spending the night alone in her crate. At some defining moment, her mood shifts. Suddenly she is fascinated by what she sees, and nothing else is visible, not even me. Before the light of day, the window transforms into a mirror that reflects a distorted, vaguely recognizable image of us. She is mesmerized by what is not real, but what occupies her senses. Like my puppy that sees the reflection from the window as real, we, too, derive meaning from a perception based on a physical world that entertains our senses, rather than seeing it as a reflection of the underlying truth.

China's invasion of Tibet around 1959 threatened the core truth of the Tibetan culture. In an attempt to preserve the essence of that culture, the Tibetans whitewashed over many of the ornate paintings that still grace the walls of the monasteries today. They hoped someday to restore the value of what they covered, so they used a whitewash that was not permanent. Similarly, the meaning we assign to the outer world is like the impermanent whitewash the Tibetans used to protect their core truth. We paint over the truth with our illusions until we are ready to value truth.

Our stories are a living myth, and like all legendary myths, the personal myth is only as meaningful as our ability to go beyond the symbolism in the story. We nevertheless tell our stories of a day, week, or lifetime recounting the facts as though the story proves we exist. We look for others to witness our stories, to validate our existence. Our words become the string that ties a bouquet of our experiences together, but like the bouquet of flowers severed from the earth, once those recounted experiences are separated from us, the captured meaning is no more than a tale.

I was telling a friend about a disagreement I had with the person I was in a relationship with. She politely listened, and when I paused, she asked, "Why can't you live without the relationship?" Here I was, a woman in touch with herself, someone who has studied herself and ancient teachings, seeking truth and meaning about her life, yet I was speaking as if the perceived shortcomings of another person were relevant. I was whitewashing over the truth, the fact that I was scared. Scared to stay in the relationship and scared to leave it, I didn't know which fear was more valid. Did I have a reason to fear leaving or a bigger reason to fear staying? The answer was insignificant, because the question didn't belong to the relationship, but to me. I was giving my power to the relationship to the point that I placed a burden on the relationship.

Truth is One Lesson Ahead of Us

We look for the uncompromising inner steadiness synonymous with the awareness of heaven, but it cannot be reached through the beautiful teachings of the divine. Our anchor is inner truth found when we connect within ourselves, not truth found from a fact learned, but truth as it uncovers who we are. Truth veils itself in the life experience. All our experiences act as catalysts for truth to infiltrate our life as quickly as white blood cells infiltrate a wound. Our most noteworthy experiences happen when we relinquish our power as we search for meaning outside ourselves.

Inner truth is not absolute, which is why there is an inner push that keeps us moving. That push is the impetus from our Spirit. Sometimes a directive that comes from within, like a rock thrown into a pond, will ripple outward, creating chaos before returning to stillness. The emotional uproar, for example, when a job is lost, is part of the distillation, the movement of an experience boiled down to the stillness of inner awareness.

Frank lost his job. In an attempt to soothe his injured ego, he went out every night. His girlfriend, tired of having her boyfriend drinking every night, ended their relationship. That final stab made him realize he was ruining his life over a job he hated. From there he realized what he really hated was his fear. Truth is not found in the stillness, but by activity that fades into stillness, yet we cannot rest in the stillness. Frank channeled his effort and energy into a new business that earned him recognition in a respected business magazine as one of the top entrepreneurs in America.

When we cling to the past, wallowing in what has been lost, we lose our connection to inner truth. If we fail to keep moving, we are resisting ourselves, because the inner truth is revealed through the inner meaning of our experiences, which is why Buddha used to say, "*Charavati, charavati,*" which means "Keep moving." Similarly, Jesus said, "Be passersby." There is a distinct difference between movement and busyness. Where busyness distracts us and is resistance to truth, movement stays in sync with our truth.

"Don't give away any points," my tennis instructor yelled from the other side of the net. I did it again. He got another point when I double-faulted my serve, one ball in the net, and the second serve too far left. The score was love, thirty. I entertained my disappointment by the thought that my score, *love,* sounded like a nice consolation prize for a loser. My next thought was that surely would be nice if in life someone stood within earshot shouting, "Don't give away any points," reminding us when we are trading motion for movement. I then smiled, realizing we are always warned.

When my car needs service, a bulb lights up on my dashboard. If I am hungry, my stomach growls to let me know. When my dogs need to go out, they sit by the door. On and on, convenient indicators in life symbolize what needs our attention. When something throws us off balance, it is nothing more than a simple indication we are in need of extracting more truth from within. Rather than go within, though, we often look for meaning on the outside. "I am upset because my partner is always late when we make plans together," for example, instead of trying to understand why someone else's actions have such a profound effect on us.

Once we understand that nothing outside of us sustains a living truth, we are solaced within, and no longer need to search frantically in all directions. "There is no religion higher than truth." Where religion has become crystallized by believers' concept of God, pseudo spirituality has no concept of God. In either case, there is no longer a flow of truth. Meaning is not found in dogma. The cut, copy, and paste spiritual teachings today are often no more than taking pieces of outdated dogma and applying a charismatic figure of authority to them. The result is the birth of a guru. The fundamental religious connection to an outer god has been replaced by the teacher who becomes a god. Dependency is created, and our power is gone. *Guru* is a Sanskrit word that means "guiding light." The only true guru is found within.

The Butterfly Effect

A theory called the butterfly effect explains that any small change in one place has the ability to make a large difference in a later state. The theory was popularized by meteorological work. Edward Lorenz's theorized that a butterfly can flap its wings in one part of the world, resulting in a hurricane in another. The theory is applicable to daily living. One simple event can change our life by making a huge difference at a later date. A friend tells of the butterfly effect when he missed a test he prepared to take for years. In a small city in India, his studies at the university culminated with a test that qualified him for his degree. On his way to the test, his train broke down, and the next train was too late. His only opportunity to retake the test was one year later. To earn money while he passed the time, he took a job as a tour guide. He was doing well as a tour guide, and actually enjoyed interacting with people from all over the world, yet something was missing. His life felt vacant. Sadly he wasn't able to dismiss what he felt as disappointment from missing the test. It wasn't that simple. During a tour, he had a conversation with a stranger from America, with whom he immediately connected. They had nothing in common at the physical level, but shared the same spiritual philosophy that merged their worlds. She was taking a group of students through India, and he was assigned to her group as their tour guide. He is now living in America teaching spiritual studies in her school, where he is fulfilled beyond his expectations, and he has aided others toward the same.

It's a disservice that we are initiated into maturity with it implied that magic doesn't exist. The synchronistic moments in life are purely magical. In the above example, my friend could have avoided his disappointment by finagling a lawsuit against the train service. In the United States such frivolous lawsuits have earned it the reputation as the most litigious society. A lawsuit would have been the perfect antidote for him to avoid the uncomfortable feelings caused by the delay in his plans, when they were purposefully acclimatizing him to discomfort; a prerequisite for the discomfort of an emerging growth surge.

There is a saying that "When the student is ready, the teacher will appear." These outer teachers provide stepping stones when the current of inner truth breaks through the dam of dogma faster than we can contain it. The seemingly insignificant, unrelated events that connect us to earthly guides usually occur in the most random way. They are an unanticipated encounter we could have easily missed, if the events in a day were tweaked differently by a centimeter. For example, I met one of the most positively influential people in my life as a result of visiting my sister in the middle of the day, acting on impulse and out of the norm of my usual routine. Precisely at that moment, a friend of hers stopped by, like me, unannounced. Her friend was excited about a mystical study program she recently began. When I mentioned I might be interested in joining, she said it was too late, because after the third week, the class was closed to newcomers. She added, "You can probably get into the next class, next year." Oddly, I didn't have to wait. Acting on an unusual impulse, the teacher made an exception and allowed me in. As an aside, the woman who told me about the class dropped it a few months later.

At one time or another, we have all walked into a room and forgotten why we entered it. We feel relief when we awaken by connecting our intention with the moment. "Oh, yeah, I came in here to get my calendar." The relief provoked by the teachers on our path is similar. They help us connect an outer experience with its inner meaning by providing us a grounding link to our inner truth.

What seems like a chance meeting is a magnetic draw that brings us together through time and space. My example led me into a formal class, but the connection can be as brief as a few words exchanged between two strangers. Whatever the duration or type of relationship formed, the grounding link it provides solidifies inner knowing. It doesn't have to be a person; a single word can pull it all together. For example, I was listening to a class lecture that had nothing to do with what I was grappling with at that time, and all of a sudden, a word became a conduit, even though the topics were different. These seemingly random occurrences on our path are an outer spark of inspiration that flames the living truth within.

When another provides a stepping stone, we must remember the stepping stones that temporarily kept us above water were never meant to be used to build a temple of worship. "It is better to be born in a temple than to die in one." As soon as we become infatuated by another person, their words are the least of the impact. Consciously we might not even remember what they said, yet unconsciously we become subservient to that person's level of consciousness.

Like the hitchhiker desperate for a lift, we don't factor in the danger when we latch onto an outer authority for inner meaning.

Karma is danger in the form of the tough lessons we experience while we take our power back. The person who took our power accumulates karma as well. By collecting the adoration of others, that person has disassociated from himself, believing the power he has asserted comes from within. Energetically, both parties breathe life into a third entity, the illusion.

A Jewish folktale tells about Rabbi Loew, who created a golem, a rescuer, out of clay. He breathed life into the golem from his belief that it was real. The rabbi was so convinced the golem was alive that the golem believed it was alive, too. The rabbi was desperate to help his people. It was a difficult time in Prague for the Jews. They were being killed with no end in sight. The rabbi, who felt powerless to make a difference, wanted to stop the senseless annihilation of his people. With the golem, he thought he could make a difference by instructing the golem to kill the enemies, thereby protecting his people. The golem obediently killed the enemies.

Power without an inner connection is ruthless, though. The golem, unable to contain that much power, turned on the people he set out to protect. The rabbi was mortified by the outcome and had to put an end to the golem, because his behavior was out of control.

When the rabbi created the golem, he had etched a word on his forehead, *emet*, which means *truth*. Realizing the golem no longer represented truth, the rabbi filled in the first e, and the word *emet* became *met*, which means *dead*.

"Discovery consists in seeing what everyone else has seen but understanding it for the first time." –Albert Szent-Gyorgyi

My initial means and methods searched to find truth outside of me. I used methods cultivated for the masses, because I was never alone. I joined a group where I was comforted by fellow seekers. Exhausted from giving my power away, and no better for it, I discovered seeking was yet another illusion in which I took comfort. Discovering inner truth from an earthly perspective is anything but comforting. Outwardly it may be viewed as a period of solitude. Inwardly it can be felt as withdrawal, where the longing to grasp onto some outer meaning is overwhelming. In my case, I grasped onto an emotional state—the feeling I belonged, but like all feelings, it didn't last.

The first time I set out to write this chapter, I was filled with anger at all the people to whom I gave away my power while I searched for truth. For example, while trying to connect to my own power, I gave my power away to a cult leader, a class teacher, and fellow students I thought were more evolved. Fortunately books are usually rewritten, because on the fifth rewrite, I realized the message I was conveying in earlier versions was more about revenge, as if something had been done to me. In life there are only participants; there are no victims. Both sides energetically breathe life into the illusion that something outside of us can give our life inner meaning; otherwise, the illusion could not stay alive.

As I concluded my report on Montezuma, I noted that his revenge would not have been to conquer Cortez, but to conquer his own illusion that Cortez was greater than Montezuma himself.

KARMA IS TIME RELEASED

Be not deceived; God is not mocked: for whatever a man soweth, that shall he also reap.

—Galatians 6:7

My two sisters and I were about to meet with my mother's doctor to discuss the battery of medical tests she had recently undergone. We feared bad news, and our drive there together didn't take away our feelings of isolation. Silently and separately we headed down the well-worn path of fear we each were prone to follow under stress. The sound of the engine shutting off was highlighted by a startling bang that brought me back to the present. The sister in the back seat carelessly had thrown open my car door with little regard to the proximity of the car next to us. The parked car she hit was smaller and certainly no threat to the heavy, steel safety beams embedded within my car door. My sister's carelessness, along with her weapon of destruction, left a dent on the other car. The dent was made more obvious by the scratch, permanently engraved like a design on a metal plate.

Two weeks later my sisters and I were scheduled to meet again. The sister who was the culprit in the parking lot mishap was the last to pull up. We waited as she got out of her car. Before I could say anything, my other sister asked, "What happened?"

Irritated, she replied, "On two separate occasions this week, I came back to my parked car and found these lovely dents."

Fully amused, my other sister and I said in unison, "It looks like instant karma."

The good news is that karma has made its way into the mainstream. The bad news is it has become a trendy word used with little regard for the depth of its meaning. Usually karma, when mentioned, is retribution for a perceived harm. We find relief in the belief that somehow, some way, a person's wrongful act will be punished. Karma is perceived as a gift from the cosmos that allows us to relax in the certainty that the revenge we'd love to take on another will be done without any effort on our part. The comfort of that belief is further embellished with the thought that it will come in a manner harsher than we ourselves are capable of conjuring. The relief is fleeting, while disappointment lingers around the unknowable element of time for that karmic debt to be called in, which is really as uncertain as the means and method of payback. The fact that we relish the act of revenge and are disappointed at not being able to witness the retribution is a good indication that we have no idea what karma means. Like Confucius said, "Before you embark on a journey of revenge, dig two graves."

The reverse misinterpretation of karma is the expectation that living right will bring reward, in some cases tenfold. I knew a man who tithed ten percent of every paycheck to his church, believing he would prosper ten times what he gave, at some later date, certainly a better return on his investment than any savings account. The same man was in the process of declaring bankruptcy, with no remorse about the losses to those he owed.

While we delight in the revenge side of karma for our enemies, we like to reserve the bountiful side of karma for ourselves. There is no plea bargaining with God. Neither prayers nor acts of goodwill will stack up credits in our karma bank. In fact, action has the least impact on karma. Karma is far too complex to condense into a simple spreadsheet like an accountant uses to weigh credits and debits against each other. If there were a lord of karma, his job would be far more complicated than keeping a tally, right action under credits, and wrong action labeled as debits.

The concept of karma in the West is a derivative of an Eastern belief adapted to fit our culture. The English translation of the Sanskrit word *karma* is *action*, but the translation is not why we focus so much on one part of the meaning. Being physically oriented, we often limit ourselves to what we perceive with our senses. The illusion of karma is that it is generated by action. Since action is the most outward impulse of the inner pattern our energy follows, even the most spontaneous act is a manifestation of a deeper motive.

Our motives are like airborne pheromones that animals emit to communicate. While our actions convey one thing, our motive is energetically interpreted differently from our actions, which is why we are frequently torn by our interaction with others. We internalize self-doubt when the act was not perceived well. What we fail to consider is that our energetic motive was received and out of harmony with the act. For example, if I feel that I am not appreciated in a relationship, I have to look past my kind actions and see my underlying intention. Often it is a plea to be chosen. The motive is not love, but the need to feel loved. For example, if someone sends flowers to another person, it could be a way to express love. It could also be the hope that the other person will return that love.

Our senses may be fooled by the appearance of a good deed, but our consciousness grasps what is real. The seed of karma is in the underlying motive beneath our intentions, regardless of the action that ensues. It is easier to understand the depth of karma when we consider its meaning in conjunction with truth. "Seek truth not in mundane details of daily life, but in the essence of life itself." –B. Tosia, as quoted in Nikita Mikhalkov's 2007 movie titled *12*.

Truth is life-force coalesced with its most compatible form. The pattern our energy flows through to create the form of our experience must be compatible with our Spirit's expression. When life feels against us, we are resisting the flow of our Spirit with an incompatible pattern. A *distortion field* is a term coined to describe the persuasive ability that people with charisma have over others. In that field, reality is insignificant. When our energy is funneled through concepts not fitting for our growth, we have created a pattern out of those concepts, better defined as a distortion field, because we actually believe those concepts, despite the fact that our reality is telling us otherwise. We may wonder why our plans don't cooperate with the results we had in mind, why someone said something hurtful, or why our experiences are often painful events, but our wonder is more like a rhetorical question.

When my mother became too ill to take care of herself, I set in motion alternate plans for her care. The way I dealt with the transition from daughter to caretaker was by gathering information and taking action on her behalf. The response may seem logical, but my distortion field during an emotional crisis is in overdrive. I don't acknowledge the grave repercussions, much less give myself permission to feel vulnerable. I gain a sense of control by being a taskmaster on a mission, like a machine, and the people around me feel incompetent and unseen.

My sisters, on the other hand, dealt with my mother's decline differently and rebelled against any solicitation I made for their help. Our childhood sibling rivalry could not compare to the intense fights we experienced during my mother's early illness. We argued so much that I doubted the closeness we shared as adults. I felt unsupported, but in my distortion field, I was oblivious to the fact that I was pushing away their support.

To cheer up my mother, I decided to bring her a gift, a framed photo from the collection of photos I took in Tibet. While I looked through the myriad pictures, the one that caught my attention was not the aesthetically pleasing one that I chose for my mother. In Tibet, I went through dozens of monasteries observing the rituals and lifestyles of the various sects of Buddhism. A photo from one of the monasteries captured what left the biggest impression on me. Looking at it put my mind in a time capsule, and I was back in Tibet. In contrast to the vibrant display of color from the other photos, it was unremarkable, with the only color showing from the monks' robes as they exited a barren courtyard. They were heading back to class after completing a ritual. From a Western perspective, the ritual was a unique way of embedding knowledge. The monks went outside between each lesson, gathering in groups of three, where they debated what they learned. It was fascinating to watch the heated arguments among the men. I didn't need to understand their language, to pick up the energetic investment they each made to get a point across. Also fascinating was the way they walked away from the debate when the time was up, with no hard feelings. They went back to their class laughing; a few were arm in arm or exhibited some physical display indicating they were in unison. As I stared at the photo, my fascination morphed from curiosity about a ritual to how the monks' ritual mimicked life. The birth of realization is usually a result of a war of concepts that conflict with each other. Being at war with my sisters was an outer manifestation of an internal struggle.

The role of karma supports the flow of life by forcing us to know ourselves, which is the only way we can keep up with inner truth. The unobtainable perfection I strived for with my mother's care served as a distraction from my feelings around letting her go, along with all the unhealed parts of our mother-daughter relationship. Time was running out.

I was shopping, when a pleasant voice announced over the loud speaker, "Good evening, shoppers, we will be closing our doors in thirty minutes. Please plan your shopping accordingly." It hit me, if the time left with my mother was limited, wasn't it more important for both of us to plan that time accordingly, and I didn't mean the everyday minutiae. Did things such as the menu choices between the contending assisted living facilities really matter? Or were the debatable pros and cons I grappled with just one more nonsensical distraction from my feelings?

One of the things I did was interview my mother, just like I did with the interviewees for my documentary on death. The formal process of an interview took me, as her daughter, out of the picture. Without any preconceived audience in mind, she was suspended beyond time. Her memories flowed without any linear order. The order was the awareness she came to about her life as she was focused on death; it was unavoidable, because it impinged on the life she knew. The impromptu awareness she formed in the face of her death reminded me, once more, that in the end, all that really matters about life is how we integrate our experiences before we die. The outer action is only the supporting role for an internal process that sometimes has to culminate into a painful karmic lesson to get our attention. In my mother's case, she skirted around a lot of those lessons, which resulted in an impending painful death.

Unfortunately, we have bastardized karma as a means of weighing physical action, like a highway weigh station weighs trucks. The popularized meaning of karma does little to make us aware of our motives that are the prelude to action. We seldom peer behind the veil of karma. We get stuck on the outer action. Otherwise, we wouldn't define karma as punishment or reward, but a means of self-balancing. The pain or pleasure projected from each experience is not the purpose of the experience, since the end result of any experience is insignificant compared to the process of awareness we gather.

Focusing on the outer experience doesn't allow energy to cycle into self-realization. Self-realization opens the channel for our individualized expression, because then we are containing life-force in a compatible form. Energy comes together and adds to itself. If instead, we reconcile the outer experience with itself, similar to a garden hose that has a kink in it, life-force can't flow past the concepts we've formed to justify our actions. For example, the fund manager changes the company's accounting to reflect positive earnings; the psychiatrist prescribes the drug he gets a kickback on, rather than the competing drug better suited for his patient; the veterinarian recommends a costly surgery and follow-up treatments when neither quantity nor quality of life is the probable outcome for the pet. The insidious part is in a distortion field, every act is reconciled. There is a saying, "He who sows the wind will reap the whirlwind."

Children are too good at relating every experience to themselves. They assume if something happens, it was because of them. They lack the ability to think abstractly and integrate understanding around an experience, so they end up blaming themselves, even if not consciously. As adults, we have the ability to think abstractly. We can relate to the experience on an inner level, but often flip the coin, instead. We deflect what we don't want to take responsibility for by blaming something or someone else. In the process of separating ourselves from our experiences, unconsciously we create anxiety. The anxiety is from fear of separation.

A friend described her six-year-old daughter's ability to remember, like any other child, as minimal. My friend believes that someone who was in her daughter's life from the past has no significance to her daughter today, if she has no conscious memory of the person. While her daughter consciously doesn't remember, unconsciously, she has absorbed the essence of all her encounters. The essence of each experience is absorbed, while our memory fades the details or folds them to fit our needs. The conscious memory from each experience is not as significant as the essence. The essence is the raw material from which we shape our lives. Fear is caused when we create separation by removing ourselves from our experiences. If we use each experience as a means to gather understanding about ourselves, we develop an inner connection nothing can destroy, and we are never alone.

"The Road to Hell is Paved with Good Intentions."

Just as one rotten apple will spoil the bushel, one unconscious motive will spoil the best intentions. Karma zooms past our intentions and brings into light the motive. The path of energy designated by our Spirit is compatible with the pattern of inner truth, but when imprisoned by outer truth, the pattern our energy flows through is incompatible with who we are. "We should not pretend to understand the world only by the intellect. The judgment of the intellect is only part of the truth," said Carl Jung. Karma helps us correct the distortion, not for the purpose of gathering evidence to expose our motives to others, but for the purpose of knowing ourselves.

When I began a career in real estate, I fell in love with every aspect of the job. If you asked me to list in order exactly what I loved about it, on the top of the list would have been providing real estate counsel to alleviate the fears of my clients during a stressful transaction. In return it was good for me to witness having value to others.

Being the youngest of three children, I was never taken seriously in my family. With my clients, though, I was listened to, heard, and appreciated. Karma is never one-sided. In the process of helping others with their real estate decisions, I gained confidence. My real estate career could have been viewed karmically as a match made from heaven, since my clients and I positively affected each other. If my inner awareness kept pace with my outer proficiency, it may have remained that way, but such a thing never happens. At some point, we become mesmerized by the tangible results of our efforts. A good analogy comes from the wisdom of a decorated Naval officer speaking to his new recruits. "The ocean is like a beautiful woman; if you are not careful, it can hypnotize you. Before you know it, you've surrendered your command to the titillating pleasure of your senses."

Like a kaleidoscope that shows a different view when turned, as life moves, we are forced to view a different perspective of ourselves. If at those turning points we have lost our connection with inner truth, we use stagnant, outer conditioning as our guide. The theme song of our world is "bigger, better, more." It plays in our head when we have turned away from our own song.

I didn't identify with my Spirit, so even if I could have gone along with the concept that I had a Spirit, I quickly latched onto an identity defined by the outer structure of success. I went from genuinely caring for my clients to becoming more concerned about my own success. Success became an insatiable goal with a finish line that kept moving, always slightly out of reach. An emergency signal was finally broadcast for karma to come to my rescue.

A selfless act flips to reveal its underdeveloped underside, when motive uses the action as its disguise. The most common example is doing something kind for recognition and not out of our own volition. Most of our actions have a hidden agenda we are not conscious of, a fact that may seem harmless, especially in light of a good deed, but every unconscious action adds to unawareness. Dishonesty is not the largest factor in the equation. Unawareness distorts our creative machinery, and we wake up one day realizing we are living a life that is not ours.

We were each meant to follow the greater pattern of our Spirit, so we have a natural inclination to funnel our energy through an inner pattern, regardless of whether it is compatible with our true nature. You can observe how most people revolve their life around a routine, and although the routine may change, it is rarely nonexistent. A friend who lost her job quickly and effortlessly replaced her work routine. She remarked that it was uncanny how she turned her job search into a routine.

When actions lack awareness, the distorted patterns to which we are in servitude mold our life as if it were a soft wax. If desire is processed from our unconscious impulses, no matter how we justify our actions, our motive is instigated by the same lacking, and the outcome looks the same. For example, the person we choose to be in relationship with is no different from the one before; we are unable to alleviate our financial struggles, no matter how much money we make; we can't earn a living equivalent to our expertise; or our interactions with others are adversarial.

Karma sets out to make us whole as it entrenches us in the experiences that provide movement to free us up. At first karma occurs ever so slightly, but as we resist change, karma builds momentum until there is enough force to break us free. In life, the final thrust that breaks through resistance causes the greatest pain, since it is the thrust that catapults us into uncharted territory. The final thrust rocks our world. What seems like a sudden shift was the climax of the change that had been building momentum.

The final jolt forces us to find inner strength we weren't aware we had, which is the blessing of karma. Aspects of us that were once impenetrable morph into potential. The tenacious nature that I funneled into career success was not a bad trait, but the place where it was funneled reached its saturation point. Until I developed more of myself, I had too much energy focused on a limited outcome, like pouring ten gallons of water into a one-gallon bottle.

On the outside, everything looked the same, but in a nanosecond, everything changed. A lot of what mattered to me before that moment felt like dead weight. Just as a sojourner may choose to leave behind the weight of unnecessary backpack items as the journey demands more of him, I left behind the weight of concepts that no longer lent meaning to my life. In my physical world, dropping the extra weight translated into leaving behind a successful career, because the inner fulfillment was long gone from it. When people emerge from an internal shift, they ask, "Who am I?" and "What is the purpose of it all?" Until we dig for the answers again and again, we are prone to follow a repetitive pattern based on a distortion of inner truth, not the inner truth compatible with our Spirit.

Dissolving anything that gets in the way of inner truth is karma's only concern. Everything else becomes expendable, even physical life. While karma can mobilize us forcefully, it is also the benevolent teacher that wants us to succeed. Before it ups the ante on the intensity of life lessons, we are given mercy in the form of synchronicity. For example, we might have a chance meeting with a person out of character from the people we know. An opportunity we never considered might seem to fall in our lap. A book with the message we need to hear might be mentioned as loudly as if it were calling our name.

Karma never impedes freewill. At some level we may at first choose to say "No" to what is put before us. If we fail to allow synchronistic events in our life, though, the rescue mission of karma changes form and becomes the harsh lesson we can't avoid. There is a point of no return, where whatever threshold we choose to cross won't eliminate the lesson. Often we second guess our choice when it opens the door to heartache. "If only I hadn't gone on that trip." "Why didn't I take the first job?" "Why did I end the relationship with her?" The momentum of force headed our way was set in motion long before the final decision we want to blame.

Karma is the king of fire. It is the hard-and-fast mentor of the evolution of consciousness and responsible for the experiences that burn through our resistance to impel inner growth. Just as it is difficult to see beyond the smoke of fire, it is difficult to see the meaning of our pain while immersed in it. We are not supposed to. We are meant to be consumed by the destructive experience. Since we are easily distracted, we would miss the purpose of the lesson if we weren't overcome with discomfort.

While the fire of karma has a reputation for punishment, once the blinding smoke evaporates, the contrast provides more clarity than before. The new horizon becomes a welcome landscape we suddenly have the courage to explore.

My barometer for a good movie is when I am so consumed by it that I am not thinking about anything else. The problems of my life don't seep in and distract me from being fully engaged while watching a good movie. When the movie is over, I leave the theater feeling a little different. For example, the parking lot is not the same as it was. It is almost as if I have a heightened awareness to everything around me, because for a couple hours everything around me was nonexistent.

It is impossible to decipher the full meaning of a karmic lesson immediately, especially while we are consumed by the experience. The search for a quick answer is based on a need, and not full disclosure. When our life feels out of control, we use the finiteness of a conclusion to steady our gait, like the railing we grab while walking up a flight of steps.

My doctor's prognosis of cancer in 1996 consumed my thoughts. When cancer didn't take my life, though, the energy freed from the relief energized my feeling of being cheated. No profound epiphanies compensated. I tried to eke out premature life-changing wisdom, attempting to make cancer payback for something. What I discovered is that the learning made available from a karmic lesson is time-released. In time, the karmic fire simmers and cooks a lifelong stew of wisdom.

Not Every Martyr is a Saint

Karma does not contain the characteristics of martyrdom. It is never by happenstance that we are involved in another person's lesson, or that others are involved in ours. When paths intersect, no prisoners are taken. The people and circumstances of one's life are magnetically drawn together. Different levels of consciousness meet in the outer world for refinement.

While the woman and I boldly walked through the unlocked gate into the back yard, there was no indication we should be cautious. She, several steps behind me, managed to escape, when our surprise attacker pounced on me like a lion.

While I dangled on the edge of life, it was amazing to me how many simultaneous thoughts could go through my mind at one time, like surround sound in my head. None of them were similar to what I would have expected, such as, "I love you, Mom" or "Lord, forgive me for my sins." Some of the ones I remember as I was being mauled by the wild beast were "Turn your head, turn your head; if you survive, faces are much harder to surgically reconstruct than limbs." "Oh, my God, I am going to die." "I can't believe I survived cancer to be killed by a dog one year later." "I know I was planning to get out of this business, but this is not the how, when, or why I had in mind."

If thoughts could have exclamation marks, this one would have had one: "What the hell is the other woman screaming about, when she is not the one being eaten alive?"

A month or so after the dog attack, I received a call from my attorney saying, "Ms Wellman, I spoke with Ms Burke, the woman who walked into the rear lot with you when the dog attacked you. Before I share what she said, you need to know it is irrelevant to your case." When I heard it was irrelevant, I went back to looking over a sales contract on my desk. His voice continued in the background, but my focus was not on his words. Occasionally I interjected an "Ah hum."

His call didn't strike me as noteworthy until he said, "She said you both walked to the back yard of the home for sale, and when you saw the dog, you started screaming bloody murder, which is why the dog attacked you."

I knew I had not heard him correctly and scolded myself for not giving him my full attention. I said to myself, "Sofia, you better pay attention; you are not hearing him at all."

He went on with the same nonchalance. "Don't give it another thought; I see this all the time. Fortunately in your case it is irrelevant."

"What? Don't give it another thought?" I was obsessed with it for weeks. I couldn't understand. No one was blaming her for the dog attack, and she had nothing to gain by lying. Why would she lie? Then it hit me. Maybe she wasn't intentionally lying, but unconsciously blaming herself. Perhaps she believed she was at fault because she screamed.

Either curiosity or insanity got the best of me, and I had to ask the woman, my witness, about her memory of the event. She must have told herself that version over and over, to the point that she actually believed it. She was vehement as she said, "I would never have done anything to call attention to you, which is why I ran out as quickly and calmly as possible to get my husband's help."

When we build a façade to validate who we think we should be and how life should unfold, we interpret everything that happens to fit behind the façade. What doesn't fit becomes distorted to fit. The distortion is always the truth—not necessarily the truth about what occurred, but how we internalize the outer event. She saw herself as a good person, which to her meant never causing harm. For her, perhaps, the karmic lesson would have been to see how hard she is on herself. She was scared and had an unrealistic expectation of how she should have reacted. Sadly, renouncing ourselves is the biggest form of blasphemy, because we sacrifice our essential nature for the conditioning that separates us from our Spirit. In the process, we separate ourselves from others. The exclusion clause we unconsciously state is that we are not like anyone else, and we have to keep our distance so our cover isn't blown.

See You in the Next Life

Once while in a heated argument, I made a dramatic exit with these words: "See you in the next life!" I puffed up my chest because I was above continuing the fight, or so I thought. Still, I was convinced the person I was fighting with would be in my next incarnation, because our relationship was tumultuous. We all suffer the Cinderella syndrome that with the "right" person, our relationship would be fairy-tale perfect. The right person, however, is the one who ruffles our feathers.

A chicken farmer told me the literal meaning of "ruffle your feathers." He said, "You can't miss it when chickens get upset. Their feathers are ruffled, but why they're upset is not always obvious." We know when someone has "ruffled our feathers," but the reason is not always obvious. The *why* unravels over time, like an old sweater, and is karma.

As much as we like to believe the romantic notion that the individuals with whom we have intense connections were with us in past lives, the truth is that we are drawn to the energy frequency of others. For example, when a mason lays bricks for a house, it doesn't matter if the bricks came from a local distributor or were imported from Spain. Although the mechanical procedure may vary slightly, based on the formation of the brick, either type of brick will allow him to complete the job of covering the wooden frame.

People stuck in destructive relationships sometimes hang on by the thread of karma to justify being together, thereby missing the lesson of growing past the point of their union. Just as the color of the brick is not important to the brick mason, we can learn the necessary lesson with any person who resonates at the required frequency. It gets tricky, because at the level of soul, we are all connected through consciousness as one totality, so it can be said in truth that we are all connected, and it would be accurate at a soul level. At the physical level, where exclusivity is maintained, two personalities projected by their individual souls and drawn together may never have been incarnated at the same time prior, yet they fit a part for each other's growth perfectly. The situation is no different from when a director casts actors for a movie. She may have a particular actor in mind for a role, but if that actor is not available, she will find another to fill the part.

I knew someone who could provide past-life information. In doing so, he was able to pick up on the energy of the circumstances of a past life and bring it into form based on his interpretation of it. For example, two people in a relationship can ask about their past life together and be given seemingly valid information relative to their current situation. As they are incarnated today, they may have never crossed paths in the past, but they provide the fertile soil for each to learn, based on where they are in their individual growth and in relation to each other. What feels like a deep connection that can be rationalized as a continuation of life together from past incarnations may be nothing more than a perfect fit to inspire the evolution of consciousness for the individuals involved. We don't need to recreate a current life with someone from a past life to be freed of the fetters of learning.

Two Magic Words

When my nephew says, "I'm sorry," he really is saying, "Please don't punish me." The words *I'm sorry* are not a karmic pass, eliminating a karmic debt.

Forgiveness, in respect to karma, is a contradiction to the guilt we burden ourselves with in life. I met a man whose wife and children had been murdered by his best friend. When I met the man years later, he had just come from the killer's execution. Among the many questions I had for him, the one that stood out the most was whether he could forgive the man who murdered his family. He said, "Christ, our lord and savior, taught us to forgive. I forgive him." As he recounted the story of the murder for me, he lingered on all the ways he believed he could have made a different outcome. Clearly, in his version of what happened, he had not yet forgiven himself. At some level he blamed himself for the death of his family; therefore, how could he have forgiven the murderer? With forgiveness there is no blame. Blaming another or ourselves is a way to massage our pain, and for a while it may work, until the burden of blame becomes too great. Letting go of being wronged or wronging another is not what frees us. Forgiveness does, and forgiveness is beyond our intellectual capacity. It is beyond an emotional exchange. True forgiveness forms at the level of knowing, the level we reach after we heal an aspect of ourselves as a result of the cataclysmic life experience.

I had a friend who served time in jail. His real crime was selling drugs, which put him in the wrong place at the wrong time, but drug trafficking was not his conviction. He was arrested as a suspect for a murder he didn't commit. He was so angry at the injustice that all he could do was obsess about how he was wronged. With nothing but time on his hands, he replayed the events that led him behind bars and relived the anger that matched his perceived injustice. The only break he foresaw was the upcoming trial, where he could be vindicated and freed. The trial was first delayed three months. It was delayed a second time for two months. The third delay had no set date. He couldn't contain one more letdown. My friend was never a religious man, but he fell to his knees. He wasn't looking for any favors from God. He surrendered with remorse, and he sobbed about the mess *he* made of his life. The very next day, he was unexpectedly released from prison. There was no bail to pay. Not even a trial lingered on the horizon, because the real felon was caught. The way he likes to describe it is by saying, "When I let go of all control and surrendered to the situation, I was freed. It was a miracle."

I met him long after he served time in jail. His life was nothing shy of miraculous. The self-growth and healing he sought was kicked off with gratitude. He said the hardest part of his story was not the time he served in jail, but the self-made prison he created from regret, guilt, and shame. It took him a while to heal. Since then he has gone on to help other people with addictions make a better life for themselves. The miracle he referred to in his story, I call karma. When the lesson is learned, karma doesn't stick around continuing to inflict pain. Often we are the ones who continue the pain long after it is useful. Who knows, maybe regret, guilt, and shame are the offspring karma leaves behind for us to raise.

What Happens in Vegas, Stays in Vegas

The motif of karma is, as the saying goes, "You can run, but you can't hide." While it can appear as though we have gotten one over on life, karma can't be fooled. It reminds me of Las Vegas, where you can bet against the house for only so long. Everyone who has gone to Vegas will start stories about how much they won, and then tell how they lost it all, often leaving out "and more." The "and more" is a good comparison of the exponential power of each cycle in life, where the lessons to learn are more potent when we have failed to apply our awareness to understanding ourselves.

The force of life—energy—cycles, so it makes sense that karma does the same. A lesson learned on one level is taken to a deeper level, where the initial learning is challenged to instill a more in-depth understanding. For example, ten years after cancer, I had another health scare that required a biopsy to rule out cancer. Ten years after the Rottweiler attack, I was attacked once again; this time by an eighty-pound giant Schnauzer. Ten years after losing a huge amount of money in the stock market, I was stranded holding a real estate investment because of a downslide in the housing market. Ten years after almost being caught by the gunshots of a crazed man, I barely missed being sandwiched between two cars that collided while I was on foot. The immutable law of karma loses its potency when we not only assimilate the lesson it was sent to teach, but also apply what we learn about ourselves. Because integrating the lesson moves us on a different path, we are no longer at the same address where the karma was initially sent. If one moves and mail is forwarded to the new address, it takes longer to be delivered, and in the case of time-sensitive material, such as karma, the delivery loses its impact with the delay.

In each of the succeeding events I described, the impact was far less, but the reminders were a symbolic representation. I am remind-ed that if I don't consistently monitor the motives behind my choices, my intentions get muddled, and my actions often are a reaction. Whenever I act out of need, regardless of how self-sacrificing it looks in the outer world, I am sacrificing inner development by supporting the autonomic rhythm to which I am most accustomed, for getting the need met in the outer world.

"The spirit of man when in nature feels the ever-changing conditions of nature. When he binds himself to things ever-changing, a good or evil fate whirls him round through life-in-death." –The Bhagavad Gita 13:21

Destiny is the accumulation of karmic lessons failed in prior lifetimes. If a person dies with the concepts that limited growth in one lifetime, the limitation will continue into the next incarnation, even if the circumstances are different. The difference in appearance is the outer changes of one incarnation to the next. For example, compared with those in our family lineage before us, we may be more educated, earn more money, have the support to leave a difficult marriage, deal with our feelings more, on and on. The lists of comparisons are endless. The danger is when we believe that those differences stop us from repeating the patterns of our lineage. Progress often is not the result of a more-evolved consciousness, but the progression of the collective consciousness as it survives a generation, energetically more empowered from the growth of the planet.

Evolution is infinite expansion. Scientifically it is viewed as the process of tangible form from a prior state to the present state. No different, the evolution of consciousness is the process of increased awareness from a prior state to the present state. There is never a point of completion. Enlightenment is not finite. It is a better-lit view of who we are along the way. With each expansion in awareness, we are challenged by a more luminous spectrum of light. As Carl Jung said, "One does not become enlightened by imagining figures of light, but by making the darkness conscious." The brighter the spectrum of inner light that shines, the more visible the contrasting darkness of the shadow we avoid. Since those undeveloped aspects hold the power of our expression, karma is the mentor of our evolution and empowers us by trying to make the darkness conscious.

Imagine what happens when the child who never could read well discovers as an adult that he has dyslexia. He then goes through training, overcomes his learning disability, and finally functions in a literate world. The world opens up to him, and all possibilities are given to him. I have a friend to whom this happened, and after teaching herself to read despite dyslexia, she graduated from medical school. She has since had a positive effect on the world by ensuring medical residents get learning tools that help them grasp the knowledge they need, to become doctors. Our true nature is buried in the darkness of unawareness that we conquer. How we implement that nature in life becomes our contribution. The greater the expedition of overcoming unawareness, the more our Spirit is revealed, and more power is generated in our actions, providing a greater, positive impact in the world.

OUR THREE BEARS

"Ahhh, this chair is just right," Goldilocks said with a sigh. But just as she settled down into the chair to rest, it broke into pieces!

—Goldilocks and the Three Bears

Every psychic, card reader, and astrologer gets bombarded with questions about romance. "When will he come into my life!" "Is she the one?" "How can I get him to notice me?" As a young girl, I searched for similar answers about imaginary love while pulling apart the petals of a dandelion, alternating with each pull, "He loves me; he loves me not."

Greeting card companies, florists, and chocolate manufacturers see a spike in consumer demand on February 14. One of their biggest money-making holidays validates the inexhaustible striving for love. It is no coincidence that songs that celebrate love sprint to the top of music charts, books with romantic undertones become best-selling novels, and movies that feature love have longevity at the box office. Drenched in romance, our culture is saturated with the message, which began with childhood fairy tales, proclaiming romantic love as the key to "happily ever after."

Falling in love, getting married, and having children is as commonplace to the cycle of life as are the months on a calendar. Why is something so deeply seated in our collective unconscious, a topic given this much attention, so elusive? Even the weak spirited who give up easily when faced with obstacles are not waylaid by love gone bad. When failed lovers are given another chance at love, contrary to their experience, they can't shake off the expectation that love equates to living "happily ever after."

When I was young, I knew Santa Claus didn't exist, but refused to swallow that dose of reality by instead choosing to believe in a fantasy that kept the magic of Christmas alive. Could it be we cling to the fantasy of romantic love because we have misplaced the magic of existence? The ethos of love gives us a glimmer of hope. Romantic love gives us an optimistic feeling, but no matter how powerful or promising, feelings won't rescue us. We may cling to an emotional state, such as "in love," but all emotional states reside near their counterparts. Only a razor's edge separates the pleasure of love from heart-wrenching pain.

Unlike the sculptor who intentionally whittles away the expendable material blocking her vision, by happenstance we whittle away the fantasy of love before we discover it is the expendable material blocking our view of love. Each cycle of romantic love acts as a chisel that removes another layer of the fantasy that began the cycle as irresistible hope. Romance promises an end to the loneliness that runs deep within us all. Even magical moments expressed by tears of joy, such as the presence of a natural wonder or the birth of a child, don't permanently keep loneliness at bay. Constant busyness helps us forget, until we hit a lull and loneliness surfaces once again. On the other hand, the passion of love gives us a sense of completion otherwise absent. Falling in love endows us with enough stamina to conquer the beast of loneliness. Being in love is a magical elixir so powerful that when it wears off, all we can think about is how we can gulp love's sweet, intoxicating, nectar once again. Each cycle of love completes a full turn, and the next cycle begins at the point of departure from the one before. Eventually the wisdom gained through our experience with love proves to be more sustaining than the surge of energy that being in love promises.

Anytime we disburse our energy without introspection, we have expended it frivolously. While we can justify the payment for a necessity, it is difficult to continuously pay when we have nothing to show for it. "How could I have wasted so much time with him?" is a comment frequently said before we own the experience of a broken heart. The surge of energy felt under love's spell feels like a debt, when the spell is broken. The self-awareness the relationship generously offered is difficult to process when our heart is broken. Not until we recognize that the in-love experience provided a lesson necessary for our growth do we get to stamp the debt paid in full.

Learning is not always monumental. Sometimes it is a minor sanding that smooths the ragged edges of a principle, a refinement as the last vestige of unawareness on one level of growth. For example, an emotionally painful experience may lead us to develop compassion for others faced with emotional pain. If we notice only the tangible results of the experience, however, such as love is lost, it isn't probable that growth will tally more than the debt of pain, which is why love has a reputation for being unfair.

Part of the irresistibility of love is the element of scarcity embedded deep within the fantasy. Its fleeting nature stimulates the same desperate grasping that a nicotine addict has when desiring a cigarette, after being forbidden to smoke. We can't criticize anyone for running toward the experience cloaked in the promise of being able to quench an inner longing in a way that nothing else can. The portal we run through for love is more embellished with hopefulness than any conscious objection standing in the way. Love is a beautiful, irresistible temptress that promises the unspoken covenant of everlasting fulfillment. As with all things too good to be true, it comes with a sense of urgency to act immediately. We must enter some opportunities for growth drunk with determination to push past logic.

Contrary to the myth of love, love is not what completes us. What completes us is the journey we take in the name of love. There we find the essential parts of ourselves that accumulate into wholeness. Ironically the significant part of love's journey begins when we awaken to find the pleasure of love has turned into the equally intense, but opposite emotional sensate state of pain. As said best in *The Wizard of Oz*, "Hearts will never be practical until they are made unbreakable."

The contrast of intense pleasure with equally intense pain is the formula behind the power of love. The greater the pleasure we derive from love, the greater the potential for pain. The opposing forces of pleasure and pain are as benign as two sticks before they are rubbed together to ignite a flame. The friction from the dueling sides of the spectrum is the fire of passion that ignites in us a momentous force we call desire. At the physical level, we feel expectation in the undying need for another person to complete us. The demand we place on others for our wholeness appears active, but expectation is a passive stance that disempowers us. If we were empowered at the moment of choice, we probably wouldn't choose to step on the "in-love" roller coaster so quickly. Not until you get off the ride can you look back at the loops of twisted metal and connect the stomach-turning excitement to the tangible movement of the ride. Love's active journey that empowers us begins when we look back to understand why we gave our heart away so freely, when we otherwise tread cautiously in life. We usually don't question our actions until the consequences of our actions turn out differently from what we anticipated. We are quick to condemn our choice in a romantic partner, but the same gift can be wrapped many ways. Given our level of awareness, a different choice on the surface will provide the same lesson that pleads to get our attention, pushing us further into self-awareness. Different actions are not what give us different outcomes; it is when we are different that outcomes change.

After many failed relationships, I was convinced there was a formula for making better romantic choices. The next time love lured me, I promised myself I would stay steady and proceed with caution. When I found myself romantically attracted to a good friend of my sister's, I took a compatibility pulse. I figured the people who knew me the best could be more objective than I about my new love interest.

I began by asking my sister, "What do you think about my asking out so-and-so?"

She was ecstatic and enthusiastically said, "I was hoping you two would get together. You will be a perfect match; you are very similar."

I then asked a mutual friend of so-and-so the same question. He replied, "Oh, no; I can't see it. You are too different."

So-and-so and I were in the same self-help class, so I asked the instructor of the course, "What do you think about my asking out so and so?" She responded emphatically, "Yes, it is perfect! You complement each other."

I then asked my psychic friend, who did not know so-and-so, "What do you pick up on my asking out so-and-so?"

He responded nonchalantly, "Well, it won't last long, but you will have lots of fun." Never ask a psychic a question, if you are not prepared for a particular answer.

The consensus about my asking out so-and-so came back with a fifty-fifty probability of its working. The coin toss was not the reassurance I set out to find. Regardless of the criteria we use to walk through the "in-love" journey, consciously we will not make our acquaintance with reason, because logic and love don't associate with one other. Picking better partners is not a skill that can be cultivated, like picking the right wine to accompany a meal. Neither can it be analyzed like a company's prospectus before making an investment.

We believe we are attracted to a person in a romantic relationship, but it is not the person per se, but to the person's unconscious pattern that coalesces with our unconscious pattern. The object of our desire projects balance to our imbalance. The greater the inner imbalance, the deeper we feel the connection toward the person who equalizes the asymmetrical aspects of our psyche, but the potential turmoil is greater, too. Since only the tip of the giant internal iceberg is processed at the level of the conscious mind, the phenomenon of attraction makes it impossible for us to consciously identify the reason for our attraction to another. Usually the more we are infatuated, the less we are able to articulate why. For that same reason, when someone is speaking of an ex love, it is not unusual to hear, "He was different when we met" or "I had no idea she was so possessive" or "He became angry."

In ancient Greece the families of the bride and groom arranged the marriages. A caste system typically dictated the arrangement. In a culture that generally acquiesced to the men, the groom's lack of control over the choice was a valid concern for the families arranging the match. Their concern was that if he didn't like what he saw before the wedding was sanctioned by the laws of the church and state, he could reject his bride; hence the bridal veil. Today we see the bridal veil as a traditional ornament to the wedding gown, but it originated in ancient Greece as a matter of practicality. It hid the bride's face, keeping everything orderly until it was too late for the groom to walk away. Similarly, the veil of karma camouflages the unconscious hook that draws us to a specific person. It forms feelings too intense for us to turn away, much less rationalize the attraction. The control we believe we exert over a choice in partners is the smoke and mirrors of the conscious mind. Conveniently any red flags waving in front of our conscious mind at the start of the relationship are exchanged by our unconscious mind into starting flags on the road to "happily ever after."

With every relationship I entered, I can remember the distinct moment I was enchanted by love's spell beyond any conscious reasoning. On a conscious level my beloved's action seemed so mild that the power it had on me was baffling, but the cryptic message I could not consciously understand clearly spoke to my unconscious. The archetype of love is not universal. It is subjective to each individual. I was drawn to a particular way my love interests smiled, sang, gestured, or responded to something I said. What I didn't realize was at that moment, I signed an unconscious contract with my beloved, and it was sealed by the signature of karma.

The love we believed was magical, a gift sent to us from the cosmos, stumbles on the mundane. "What? You are going golfing, when we haven't spent any quality time together in weeks?" "Since when was a new dress in the monthly budget?" "Why won't you share your feelings with me?" "If you don't stick up for me the next time that evil woman you call your mother puts me down, I'm leaving." "Can't you see how hard I am working to make a better life for us?" Power struggles surface when the reason we are there unveils itself after having waited for the most opportune time to make its presence known. The contrast between how it was and how it became makes us feel we were deceived. It is simpler to conclude that the other person miraculously changed than to admit we purposely, but unconsciously, deceived ourselves. The characteristics that repel us from another were always there, but were originally preempted by the binding attraction of an unconscious pattern. There reaches a point in the relationship when we find ourselves wondering who we are with, and that is the time we need to face the reason we are there. Since our unconscious is efficient, neither time nor space gets in the way of its ability to process a moment. Whatever is happening in the present links into a history of lifetimes. The reaction, reinforced by repetition, is the one that surfaces. Although it may or may not have been a wrong response in the past, the same reaction meant to keep us safe from wild beasts in the external world separates us from facing our internal beasts. Instead we fight or flee the relationship through battles about money, sex, children, or something else.

Goldilocks and the Three Bears is a good analogy for romantic love. When we seek in another the aspects of ourselves that we either disown or never developed, we become like Goldilocks, who was determined to find comfort in a house that was not her own. Like Goldilocks, who fell asleep in one of the beds belonging to the three bears, we slumber in the emotional state of "in love," believing we can rest there peacefully, as if life will remain static from that moment on. Like Goldilocks, who was awakened by the three bears, however, whenever we slumber in the emotional state of in love, our three bears of fear, doubt, and insecurity wake us up to face the fact that nothing outside ourselves will make us complete. They make their presence known when life moves and we haven't moved with it. In those moments we ask questions like, "Why didn't he call me?" "Does she like someone else?" "What did he mean when he said that?" "Does she really love me?"

Just as the three bears in the story meant no harm to Goldilocks, the three bears of fear, doubt, and insecurity aren't there to harm us. Neither are they there to end our relationship. They are symbolic of where we need to reflect on our actions, using our reactions as a question mark. When we find aspects of the one we love less than favorable, the orphaned aspects of us are ready to come home. Usually the arrival of the three bears alerts us to focus on the relationship, but the time is best served focusing on ourselves. Our three bears of fear, doubt, and insecurity are the conduit to our power. Like the fuse leading to a stick of dynamite, fear, doubt, and insecurity lead us to a source of inner power. If we retreat from what we don't want to face in ourselves, we manifest powerlessness, because we are destined to face who we are in another person over whom we have no control.

The tumultuousness of attraction is that unconsciously we long to merge with the same pattern we repel. Repulsion is nothing more than another form of attraction, drawing one away from one thing and toward something else. We are drawn to merge with another, but then repelled by aspects of the other person so that we can merge with ourselves. Unconsciously we seek a partner who reflects the qualities we do not identify with, but possess as we strive for wholeness. An intimate relationship is the difference between seeing our reflection in a small bathroom mirror over the sink versus seeing it in a full-length mirror on the door, yet when the full-length mirror reflects what we don't want to see in ourselves, it is easier to shatter the mirror—that is, criticize the other person—than it is to face ourselves.

Until I was able to access my anger, the relationships I attracted were with people who were overtly angry. While I criticized the expression of anger in my partners, through these relationships, where anger was accessible to my partners, I learned the ability to express it for myself. The reason I could not express my anger was insignificant and possibly a product of past lives and not necessarily this one short life. My anger was there, but I suffered anxiety and depression from turning it inward. Soon I found the opposite side, or the expression of anger, was no more constructive for my life. In fact, in subsequent relationships I expressed my anger too willingly. I had to develop the balance between turning it inward and express-ing it outwardly. Today my anger, when in balance, is transformed into a force that pushes me through obstacles. Even when we develop parts of ourselves as the result of the interaction in a relationship, it is still up to us to polish the newfound gem and place it in the setting most fitting for our own life.

I didn't have a flash of inspiration one day and say, "I'm picking angry partners because I can't access my anger." Self-realization is never a straight line. We become brave and we become scared. We take three steps forward, two steps back. The back and forth flattens out the weeds in our way so we can forge forward. Part of the evolution in the cycle of love is seeing where the other person ends and we begin; otherwise, the support with which we could have grown from becomes an enemy on a mission to conquer and destroy. We create the effect of an autoimmune disease that attacks our body's tissue, when we attack or try to change a partner, because we are really attacking ourselves. Growth cannot happen in a hostile environment.

Certainly lifelong commitments such as marriage are not wrong, and neither are attempts to form lasting love relationships, but given the level from which the commitment originates, it shouldn't seem astounding that we live in a society with a fifty percent or higher rate of divorce. It is a travesty that divorce is judged harshly, but the collective illusion that relationships and marriages are built upon are seen as something that must be protected at the expense of the individuals. Often painful endings are the thoroughfare to finding wholeness before we can form a lasting relationship.

By the way, it is interesting that marriage, which is referred to as an institution, is far from being organized as one. Typically an institution is built on clearly set forth principles and agreements. Because most love relationships are formed at the level of the unconscious, usually neither participant in the institution of marriage is conscious of the underlying principles that form the basis of their marriage. If the partners were aware, they probably would not be so eager to march down to the altar of matrimony. Rather than marriage vows, what they would recite might sound something similar to this: "I, Stephen, take thee, Sharon, to nag me daily, aiding and abetting the constant guilt I feel about not doing enough for those who are significant to me. In return I will ignore you when you need my attention, which will add to your feeling of worthlessness and abandonment."

On a conscious level we believe we are searching for a partner who meets the criteria of compatibility, such as similar beliefs, likes, goals, and lifestyles, which are essential for day-to-day harmony. Often when we find this individual, we label him or her as friend. Rarely is this person a lover. The person we fall in love with doesn't score well on compatibility after the initial wave of lust wanes. Just as one would be bored repeating the same grade in school over and over, we would lose the compulsory intrigue that causes us to merge our life with another person's life if there were nothing to learn.

Relationship harmony is not a constant state of perfection, but an equal state of tension between the energies of the involved individuals. Otherwise, one or the other dominates, rather than forming a harmonious union wherein each person expands from the contrast of the other. One of the biggest lessons for me in relationships is realizing that if the energies are disproportionate, we do not internalize growth along the way. For example, if one person pursues and the other runs, or one person gives and the other takes, then we fuel a pattern of inertia weighted down by our resistance to grow. Inevitably the relationship comes to a dramatic crescendo manifesting as an external event. At a pivotal point, the pattern is blown apart, and the individuals feel their lives have been shattered. An affair is an example of a pivotal point. A troubled relationship is difficult to retrofit into harmony if the combined energies of the individuals are accustomed to fueling the pattern of inertia, which is almost always more comfortable than change. Often without realizing it, the couple desperately tries to reconstruct the old pattern, when, for example, one person is blamed for the affair.

Mark had an affair three years into their marriage. He never meant to be unfaithful, and he wondered if he would have gone through with the infidelity if he hadn't been drinking. He wasn't proud of his answer. He didn't want his marriage to end, but he was less and less enthralled with the woman who at one time he couldn't imagine spending his life without.

Stacy was the perfect wife by all outside accounts. Mark's needs and wants were always important to her. Stacy didn't have good role models for marriage, so she made sure she understood the enormity of the marriage vows they took. She read every book she could find that defined the criteria for a good marriage. She took all the information seriously, extracting any tidbit that resounded with reason. Her friends teased her when she shared the latest discovery. That was Stacy; she didn't do anything half-hearted. When she found out about the affair, her world shattered.

I met her long after she reconciled with Mark. The year they were separated is a short blip on the radar of their long-standing marriage. What she shared, they both learned when they were separated. The image of what marriage was to them was not what either of them really wanted. Mark wasn't the only one being deceitful. Stacy resented all that she did for them. She felt lonely and empty in return, but never shared her feelings, since she believed it was part of being married. Her resentment contradicted her actions, but Mark still felt it. His translation was that he failed to be a good husband, but he brushed it off with jokes about marriage to his friends, such as "Being happily married is an oxymoron."

Stacy said that when the marriage ended, she felt like every emotion a human could feel was dumped into a blender and stirred up, and she was left the impossible task of sorting it all out. Since she was the one who always had everything in order, her ambivalence was more than she could bear. She calls it a fluke that they got back together, because when their relationship ended, love was not one of the feelings she felt. "You know it has never been easy being married, but the separation gave us the motivation to be able to figure out what doesn't work for us individually, bringing us closer to what does. Wasn't it Edison who saw himself closer to discovering electricity after failing at least one thousand times? We renewed our vows, but they were a lot different from the ones our family and friends witnessed years earlier. Our new vows place honesty and growth above anything else, which is not always easy to do or identify. The self-awareness we experience individually makes us more intimate as a couple. I call it a wish-fulfilling process, because as we become comfortable with ourselves, we communicate better with each other."

A therapist once told me the issues of a couple can't be resolved; they dissolve. I have found in some cases the issues evolve, becoming greater. Not all relationships work out. Years ago I attended a relationship workshop with a person I was dating. We attended a weekend of promise built on exercises meant to teach us how to have a "conscious relationship." No miracle relationship healing occurred over the weekend; in fact things became far worse. Instead of becoming more conscious individuals as a result of the workshop, we each felt more justified in our reactions to one another. Our expectations widened more than our conscious awareness. After all, if my partner understood the source of my reactions, not only did I expect acceptance around those behaviors, but I also believed I should be coddled. When we treat our partner like the parent who let us down, we do so with the hostility of an adult. Children are far more forgiving.

Arbitrary and untimely intimacy adds to feeling vulnerable and puts the unconscious on the defense. Try reasoning with someone who is out-of-control angry. If you go to the other person's level of anger, the fight escalates out of control. If you meet the unconscious at its level, the response is the same.

When we are more committed to the activity of our intellect and emotions than action of thought, change is not a harmonious transformation. More weight is added to the distorted pattern through which energy funnels, causing it to turn into chaos quicker. The power of what we are not conscious of is exponential, exceeding what we have the ability to comprehend intellectually or emotionally. The law of chaos is that order is always found, but not from the level it occurred. The fulcrum of harmonious transformation depends on going past the pattern dominating the individuals, not blowing it apart. The only way past the distortion in focus is to act from self-awareness brought forth each and every time we face our three bears. In that way we internalize change without external drama.

Anytime we feel fear, doubt, or insecurity, we are at risk of acting from a pattern reaction. We may not be conscious of the underlying issue, but if we become aware of how it feels in our body, the discomfort of anxiety, tension, and heaviness can be a helpful clue. When we feel such discomfort, we are pulling back the bow, preparing to pierce our target with angry words, and our love interest is often the target. With archery, energy is tensely held in the archer's quivering arm as he draws back the arrow. The bow bends and the energy transfers to the arrow, when the archer releases it. If we can hold the energy, no matter how uncomfortable it may be, like the archer does *before* he lets go of the bow, we avoid making a target out of the one we claim to love.

Until we act out our realizations without *acting*, we have not manifested change, and the unconscious pattern is in control. How well we figure it out in the aftermath is not enough. No matter how well we dust through the event with an apology, there is always a particle of distrust left behind. Worse than that, we have validated the unconscious pattern.

Our fears, doubts, or insecurities are the real threat and the target we must pierce. They corrupt the present with the past. Our parents, caretakers, past relationships, and so on are continuously brought into the relationship, adding weight onto the pattern of inertia in play. When the relationship comes apart from the weight, we are given another chance to learn more about ourselves—in the next relationship. But wait, we don't leave empty-handed; we take the three bears of fear, doubt, and insecurity with us.

It took several relationships for me to realize relationships don't necessarily end from a lack of love, but from an inability to express love. Everything is a reflection or shadow of the underlying reality. For a relationship to be unified, it must be refined through a willingness to unify oneself. If our focus is on the relationship, we are using the relationship as a way to resist inner growth. The same way rust eats away metal, resistance to growth eats away at a relationship until, like rust, the damage penetrates and becomes inseparable from the relationship it has corroded. The critical mass is the point where it is impossible to push past resistance and keep the relationship.

It is a common fact that oil and water don't mix, which is why oiling a surface susceptible to rust is a great preventative. An inner relationship is the oil that repels rust in our relationships. When we face our fears, doubts, and insecurities, we don't need our relationship partner's help pointing them out.

My relationship partners shared a character flaw—being criti-cal. After many failed relationships, I began to see the correlation between my lack of self-acceptance and their criticism. The criti-cisms were coming from my love interest, but how could I have blamed another person for energetically acknowledging my unhealed wound? The stronger my relationship is with myself, any assumptions that insinuate I am wrong are repelled by the oil of self-awareness. Self-awareness is healing. For me that healing is reflected in my life when I don't need to defend myself or blame someone else.

Blame, as a symptom of resistance, has an insidious component that deteriorates self-reflection. Recently while driving to an unfamiliar area of Atlanta, I programmed into my navigational system the address of my destination. I was distracted by a conver-sation on my cell phone, so when the mechanical voice on the navigational system told me to turn left in a quarter of a mile, I went straight, missed the turn, and had to make the nearest U-turn to get back on track. The navigational system recalculated my route to accommodate the error. The system never reflected anger toward me for the way I was driving, even when I missed another turn, yet I found myself becoming angry at the inanimate object for correcting me. Each time she said, "Make the nearest legal U-turn," I became annoyed at it, even though I was the one who missed the turn. The ridiculousness of the negative emotions I conjured toward my navigational system brought me back to reality with a smile. Feeling inadequate at my inability to follow the simple instructions guiding me, I needed to blame the system, rather than feel inadequate. How easy it is to project onto another what we don't want to claim in ourselves! We even project our inadequacies onto inanimate objects. The trap is that if I make someone else responsible when I feel inadequate, I will search for a way to feel adequate through someone else's approval. In either case, I am not free, but trapped in a pattern of inertia while avoiding inner growth.

Justification is the greatest enabler of resistance. When my sister and I spent a night in Greece drinking ouzo, the licorice-flavored liqueur that went down way too smoothly taught me a big lesson. We laughed hysterically, and then we sobbed with the same hysteria as the laugh only minutes before. While we were sitting outside enjoying the mild evening breeze from the quaint café, the activity on the sidewalk we faced was innocuous, until two men caught our attention. They were easy to spot, because as they exited the restaurant next door, they created an uproar. We didn't need to be fluent in Greek to tell the fight escalated past the point where either man was listening, as they competed to out shout the other. Something then happened, like someone pulled a switch. The fighting abruptly ceased and the two men hugged one another. Their voices fell to a whisper. They looked at each other apologetically, shook hands, hugged again, and parted ways.

In unison, my sister and I sanctimoniously said, "We're not crazy; we were just being Greek." Now, with pride, we could attribute to our lineage our ability to go from one emotional extreme to the other with the same intensity, with little time in between. Over another round of ouzo, we toasted our discovery and the people of our lineage. As I lifted my glass, I felt vindicated for any behavior I acted out. I wiped away self-responsibility like unneeded caulk on my mental caulk board.

Blame and justification obscure self-discovery with an interpretation that keeps us the same. The opacity of justification is more dangerous, because it is darker than blame. At least with blame there is an element of discomfort, since it is usually delivered with anger or sorrow. Justification doesn't see the light of day insulated in self-righteousness. If we need proof of how our unconscious masterfully creates our lives, the ease at which we paint the perfect excuse over self-disclosure is a good example. Faster than our ability to consciously register the self-deception, we have added another layer onto the pattern of inertia familiar to us.

It is better to make a mistake that results in our knowing ourselves deeper than it is to maintain the status quo. From the wisdom of Soren Kierkegaard, "To dare is to lose one's footing momentarily. Not to dare is to lose oneself."

I Love You, I Hate You. Are You My Soul Mate?

Since a soul connection is the antithesis of dependency, *soul mate* does not describe a relationship wrought with emotional angst. Loosely we use the label *soul mate* to describe a relationship that moved the underpinnings of our life just enough to have an impact on the already disturbed foundation, quickening the arrival of an emotional tsunami. The relationship was not the cause, any more than the last drop of water causes a bucket to overflow. We credit the relationship for the impact that rocked our world, because it was the point of focus when the wave of suppressed emotions crashed down. The intense feelings flowing into our life seem to have emerged from one person, but they were already there, becoming more deeply buried within our psyche each time we avoided facing our three bears of fear, doubt, and insecurity. The feelings attached to our emotional reactions can't go anywhere until they are dissipated through inner awareness. Crediting the relationship with a label beyond earthly terms is easier than unburying the aspects of ourselves we purposely avoid, even when avoidance coats future experiences in toxic residue.

The feelings we deny seep out in our actions. The anger I felt toward my sister during a disagreement spilled out, literally. As I looked at her assorted Christmas gifts displayed on the coffee table, I managed to be the klutz who spilled red wine all over them. Consciously it was an accident, but because we live on many levels of consciousness at one time, it could have been anything but an accident.

Warning: Toxic

A man who inherited property from a relative found out quickly that he inherited a problem, not a gift. It is difficult to lose someone we love through physical death, but in this instance, a difficult time became an insurmountable challenge. The land he inherited was saturated with toxic chemicals and unmarketable. The relative, who generously bequeathed the land at the time of his death, believed that if something was out of sight, it was one less thing he had to worry about. His actions coincided with his convictions, as he carelessly chose to bury old tires, oil, paint, and other toxic things, rather than dispose of the items correctly. Over time what he buried caused a toxic reaction underground, ruining the once-fertile soil. Perhaps he was ignorant about the consequences of his actions, but ignorance doesn't eliminate effects.

Any aspect of ourselves that we bury, eventually we are forced to face. Similar to the items buried underground, the longer we keep those aspects of ourselves hidden, the more toxic they are to our wellbeing. As Confucius said, "No matter where you go, there you are."

Each time we awaken to the fact that love won't shelter us from the desolate, cold loneliness at our core, we demand more from ourselves to feel complete. The expectations we have for another has less to do with them than about the way we bury our own neediness—the need to feel complete—without making the effort to embrace who we are. Everyone who enters our lives is there to teach us something about ourselves, not to save us from ourselves, because we can't escape. Relationships enter or leave our life depending on what we need for growth. True compatibility is about alchemy, not longevity.

Alchemy requires suffering, whether human beings, metals, or any other matter is forced into change. For instance, metal used to make a sword is beaten down and melted; clay to make a pot is molded and fired on a kilm; stone to build a column is broken and fastened together. Two individuals who form a relationship are forced to wrestle with three bears—fear, doubt, and insecurity.

In early times, an alchemist experimented with combinations of materials by mixing substances. Not all those combinations had the potential to create gold. Relationship gold is the relationship that pushes us to know ourselves as a result of the interaction with another. It provides the environment conducive for transformation. As Carl Jung said, "The meeting of two personalities is like the contact of two chemical substances: If there is any reaction, both are transformed."

ENERGY MISDIRECTED

When I was having a fireplace installed in my studio, the installer closed off the main gas line going into my home so that he could add a new gas line leading to the fireplace. After the worker finished, rather than reopening the main gas line to resume the availability of gas to my home, the installer made a mistake that resulted in gas filling the atmosphere outside instead. Everything seemed fine until the next morning, when I turned the stove knob and nothing happened. No flame burst forth, as it normally would have. Still not suspecting the fireplace installer as the cause, I called the gas company, believing it caused the problem. An employee rushed out to my house and became legitimately concerned when he uncovered the mistake the fireplace installer made. The gas accumulating outside could easily have been ignited by any spark, even from an otherwise harmless thunderstorm. My home could have been destroyed, with me inside. Gas itself is not hazardous. It heats my home in the winter; it allows me to enjoy the cozy ambiance of a fireplace in an instant; it provides a hot shower for me in the morning; and it cooks my food. The misapplication of gas, however, can have hazardous results. Similarly, the energy as life that flows through us is not hazardous, but misdirected, it has the potential to be.

Yesterday my energy was as scattered as the gas accumulating around my house from the fireplace installer's mistake. Being scattered, my energy was potentially hazardous to the creation or lack of creation of my future. I never finished what I started, and I wasted a lot of time, going off on meaningless tangents. While researching newspaper archives for my documentary, I read about koi fish ponds, the mating practices of peacocks, and the weather patterns in Antarctica. It wasn't as bad as if I were using my energy to plot a murder, yet the intention behind my actions could be viewed as harmful. I was scattered, burned out, and in dire need of a break. I would have been more productive if I had relaxed, watched a movie or two, taken a walk, and napped here and there throughout the day. The well-needed break came with a backlog of feelings that my meaningless busyness kept at bay. Herein lies the hazard. Avoidance over time has the potential to crystallize into a pattern, creating an inflexible habit of scattering our energy.

Think about how you feel after working on a project that requires mental application. Sitting while performing the task doesn't make it any less exhausting. We do not realize how much energy thought requires, focused or scattered. While I wholeheartedly subscribe to the mind-body connection, an incident with a business partner reinforced my knowledge. We owned a home renovation business, and our combined forces complemented each other and the business. He had a ton of contacts, and I had a diverse background in real estate. The combination, coupled with our equally strong work ethic, was a winning formula for success, and we were both excited. Shortly after we began, I realized my excitement overshadowed my judgment, and I was not being realistic about time. My priorities in life had long before shifted. Where I was once focused on building a successful business, my new focus was on writing this book and producing a film. The two were huge undertakings and already in a tug-of-war over my time. There was no way I could do more and do anything well.

Gently I broke the news to my business partner, all the while I reassured him I would not leave until we completed all pending projects and he found my replacement. Part of my motivation to stay until the projects we started were completed was to protect my interest. After all, I spent a considerable amount of time on the projects we had pending.

His disappointment in my decision to leave the partnership was followed by a campaign to change my mind. He offered to do more of the work if I stayed. In theory it was a great offer, too good to refuse, but for some reason, his offer felt more like someone asking a favor when you are too busy to oblige. Even if I could determine in hours the time that I physically picked up the phone to make a call regarding one of our projects, went to a jobsite, or calculated a proposal, the total would be slim in comparison to the energy I expended being responsible for my commitment to our clients as well as to him. When he found my replacement, even though the pending jobs weren't finished, I was happy to walk away and let him have it all. It was fair to my business partner that I exited the partnership as soon as he found someone with the same goals as his—of building it into a large business. It was fair to me, too. The moment I made that decision, I discovered a reserve of energy available to me best described as relief. Clearly the physical expenditure of energy was not the problem as much as the energy I used to uphold my commitment.

Addiction

A focused expression of energy often is described as a passion for and dedication to something, which, when you think about it, is no different from the description of an addiction. If you asked most people to name addictions, they would repeat the common forms we all know, such as alcohol, drugs, eating disorders, sex, gambling, shopping, smoking, and work, yet as I write this book, it can easily be said that I am addicted to doing so. Put that way, what is the difference between my addiction to writing and someone else's addiction to drugs? I know that comparing the two sounds ludicrous. While the adjectives defining the point of distinction seem to differ only slightly and could appear to be a matter of semantics, the impact they have on our life is significantly different. One is directing energy to achieve gratification, and the other is for fulfillment. Because human beings are sensate based, we form emotional addictions to things that are gratifying.

Gratification is therefore fleeting and momentary, and when gone, it always leaves us wanting more. Like a gas tank that has a hole, there is never a satiation point.

On the other hand, fulfillment is never achieved through anything that is gratifying. Whereas gratification is led by an end result, fulfillment is led by the process of doing, bypassing a specific outcome as the motivation. The process of doing what is fulfilling connects us to ourselves. The process stems from our creative level and is in sync with the expression of our Spirit. Both gratification and fulfillment undeniably are the result of our addictive nature. Where one is energy expended toward an outward focus, the other cycles energy back to us, never leaving us energetically depleted or feeling empty in the process.

The addictive nature is part of our being, and just like the ego, it is not meant to be destroyed or eliminated. Concluding that the word *addiction* is negative is "throwing the baby out with the bathwater." The energy behind the addictive nature is very constructive, but when misdirected, it has the potential to be destructive. As with the ego, our addictive nature crosses over from helpful to hurtful, depending upon where we direct it. When we direct the addictive nature toward gratification, we create the inverse of the placebo effect, the placebo effect being where a harmless substance becomes curative because of the patient's belief that it works. The inverse is no longer the belief in a harmless substance, but the belief that without it, harm will be caused, such as the belief that life is over when a significant relationship ends.

We are meant to be addicted to our own Spirit. We don't have to go to church or synagogue every week, but we should live a life that coincides with faith; faith not as an intellectual belief, but surrendering to the patterned flow of life that cycles through us. The mold for what appears physically is cast based on our flow with or resistance to growth. Like bending a wire hanger, when we bend change at the physical level, we are saying we don't like the pattern we have directed our energy through, but rather than surrendering to our Spirit, we attempt to further impose our will to make a change at the physical level. From the physical level, our energy is not as potent as the full cycle of energy available to us when we connect within.

For example, Julie begged her husband to go into couples counseling. No matter how logical her argument was, he adamantly opposed the idea. Julie sought help for herself. Initially she went looking for a pair of objective ears to hear complaints about her marriage. The counselor was wise and shifted the focus to Julie's life, with the marriage issues as an aside. The experience created an energetic shift. Julie stretched the tight boundaries of her marriage, giving herself an opening to bring in the fullness of who she was. Once Julie began to focus on growing and improving herself, she did not mention marriage counseling anymore. After a few months, though, her husband said he was ready to go to couples counseling with her.

The Trip without a Map

A haunting echo resounds within us when we know we are on the right path in life. In 1991, I walked away from a career that had stability and benefits and walked into the unsure horizon of commissioned sales, in a field I had no knowledge about. Most people thought I was crazy, and from all logic, I couldn't deny them their opinion, though I never second guessed my decision. At other times, I have been too disconnected from myself, and I would have regarded any inner guidance or assurance as an annoying sound in the distance, until the volume turned up in the form of hardship. Despite how uncomfortably that journey into the unknown begins, we can never consciously navigate such a perfect trek. Life was on my side; on the surface it appeared as if I followed the footsteps of King Midas, because everything I touched turned into gold. In sync with the flow of my Spirit, I was fulfilled.

People think that following their divine flow has to look altruistic and it means being without. Money is a form through which energy cycles back to us, but when it becomes about the money, there is no fulfillment. When my addictive nature flipped and was directed toward gratification, everything fulfilling was gone. My energy flowed away from me, rather than cycling through me, leaving me depleted and open to cancer, among many other catastrophic maladies. We want to be addicted to what it feels like when our energy completes a cycle through us, not the short burst of energy we get from what is gratifying. Being in the divine flow gives us the energy to run a marathon, because it cycles energy back; seeking only gratification is a short sprint that quickly depletes us.

The sweet spot in tennis is where the ball and racket make perfect contact. Even if a player misses that sweet spot, the ball may still get back over the net, until the time when it doesn't. When we are in sync with the divine flow of our Spirit, we hit manifestation with a perfect punch. It is no coincidence that all twelve-step addiction-recovery programs are spiritually based programs intended to direct the addictive nature away from gratification and toward the will of a higher power. Although these programs are good at pointing the addictive nature toward faith in a power higher than the physical self, often those who attend such meetings assume the higher power is separate from the self, which results in becoming addicted to the program, rather than to their own Spirit.

Steve Jobs, the founder of Apple, made himself as an example of someone who listened to the guidance from within. He followed his passion, which on the surface at times appeared inconsequential. I heard him tell a college graduating class about following your intuition. He used his life as an example. He dropped out of college because of the financial burden it placed on his parents, but stayed and "dropped in" on the classes he wanted to learn something from—the classes he was drawn to. One of those classes was calligraphy; it had no utilitarian use for a man one step above homelessness, sleeping on the dorm room floors of generous friends. Later calligraphy proved to be essential in the advent of the computer he developed, the Macintosh. He said, "You can't connect the dots looking forward; you can only connect them looking back."

Chances are when we do something, go to AA, attend church, take a class, follow a teaching, or read a book for the purpose of finding meaning to life, rather than use that structure like a ferry boat that takes us from one side of a river to the other, we mistake the structure for the river. It happened to me. During the time I believed I was in touch with a higher authority through a spiritual leader, I negated any impulse from within. I didn't do a single thing from the impetus of my being. It was the only period in my life that I didn't take the initiative for any creative outlet, be it business, art, or athletics. I directed my focus on and acquiesced to the group consciousness in everything I did.

Still, breaking away was painful. My energy was directed to the group and had been for quite a while. All of the sudden, though, I had a surplus of energy and nowhere to put it. I didn't tread gracefully like a trapeze artist carrying a flame across a thin wire. I was more like a knight on horseback carrying a torch ready to set fire to anything in its path. I had no faith and felt like I had to find something quickly to replace the void.

The essence of faith is the inner knowing that everything in life has a purpose. The intricacies of the purpose were made more obvious as I approached recycle bins. With a bin labeled and divided by the type of material I was disposing, the simple act throwing away the remains of my lunch became a precise task. I had to separate the plastic plate and utensils from the glass bottle, and the plastic and glass from the remaining food and paper napkins. There is a recycle bin between manifestation and our Spirit, where the essences of our experiences get recycled back to us in the form of energy, but how we use the energy depends on our relation to the experience. If a personal connection is made with our experience, we forge a connection with the wisdom of our Spirit; otherwise, the experience recycles back in the form of a similar experience. The former is fulfilling; the later leaves us wanting something more.

Life has a forward thrust, so if we aren't energetically connected with the flow of our Spirit, we feel like an empty space is left behind. Our natural inclination is to fill that space. Seeking gratification is a knee-jerk emotional reaction to the void, but since anything gratifying is fleeting and momentary, we are quickly brought back to the emptiness.

Unconsciously we are programmed to "need" whatever once filled the emptiness, even when the cost to do so is obviously destructive. We direct energy away from us, rather than cycling it through us, where we connect with our Spirit. In this way, we create addiction.

An Impossible Promise

A tenant wrote me bad checks in excess of $1,600. Writing bad checks constitutes a felony in Georgia, so in response, I took out a warrant for his arrest. The morning of court, he arrived with a money order to clear up the matter, but we still were obligated to go through the procedure to have the charges against him dismissed. Before the case was called, we were forced to witness several cases ahead of ours. The cases varied, some being more serious than others.

With the more severe cases, the perpetrator was brought in from jail handcuffed and shackled. One man up on charges of domestic violence allegedly was responsible for severe lacerations to the back of his girlfriend's head. He appeared before the judge in a remorseful posture with head bowed. The judge let him out of prison until the later trial, but first she made him promise he would not go near his girlfriend. Her words exactly were, "Even if she calls you and says, 'Oh, babe, please come see me,' do not go near her."

I was horrified with the judge's decision. Because of the apparent nature of the relationship, I knew the minute the offender got out, he would attempt to see his girlfriend, offering apologies, pleading, and promising that he had changed. She probably would consent to see him, in lieu of experiencing the void she was feeling in his absence. The mold of their pattern, though mildly stretched during the time they were apart, would return to its original shape, with violence as part of the picture, until the energy was too much for the pattern and a final violence escalated to a horrid ending. We all know of stories of abused women going back into abusive relationships, only to be maimed or murdered. Addiction to an outer source is at the core of the pattern.

When we are addicted to gratification, we desire to change when the result of our addiction becomes destructive, but our desire for change becomes part of our delusion that adheres us to the addictive cycle. Talking about change becomes part of the energetic fuel the addict needs. There are people who carry on about the negatives in their relationship, yet make no move to change. While the impetus to change is nonexistent, the expression of the desire to change becomes a way to quiet the inner voice that knows. All the while, it is energetically gratifying to talk about a negative relationship, because it solicits others to give energy to the person addicted to the relationship. When we aren't cycling energy within, we seek energy from without, to fill the inner void. Emotional stimulation is energy, whether it is given in concern or anger or through a scenario that causes emotional and sometimes physical angst.

Like someone on drugs for years, someone with an emotional addiction after a while loses the impetus to make life different, because the pattern is too deeply ingrained. Although there is always hope for change, the likelihood becomes less, with time. The longer the sensate nature rules over consciousness, the more difficult it becomes to stand up against withdrawal, because withdrawal requires that a person rule over his or her sensate nature. Similarly, if a parent does not discipline a child from a young age, the parent will have a harder time implementing authority over the child when the child becomes a teenager. The longer the lag time, the more difficult or almost impossible the task becomes.

Til Death Do Us Part

My sister informed me that my father's wife was going to leave him. After thirty-five years of a turbulent marriage, she finally had enough. My sister supported our step-mother's decision. My sister was convinced that his wife was, in fact, leaving him and gaining freedom from his oppression. I, on the other hand, was not convinced she was going anywhere, so I bet my sister a dinner at the winner's restaurant of choice. My bet, contrary to my sister's, was that my father's wife would not leave. For too long, she had programmed her unconscious that she needed the marriage, whatever the reason. Probably, as any addiction begins, the marriage was once gratifying. It temporarily filled the empty space or gap left behind when life moved forward. I can only imagine that when they met, the relationship provided a stabilizing element for her, regardless of how it looked on the surface. One month before the divorce was a reality, my father's wife fell ill and had to quit working, thus becoming totally dependant on my father. For her, unfortunately, it was too late. The underlying fear of the void she would feel without the relationship was deeply embedded in her unconscious and inaccessible to her, no doubt instilled from years of repetitively breaking up and going back. At all costs her unconscious sought the gratification that once so perfectly filled that empty space, so she manifested an illness to keep the status quo, even though consciously she expressed the motivation for change and was talking about her plans to support a change.

The bet my sister and I made is one I would rather have lost. Almost six months later, my father's wife died in her sleep. I was sad for her life, but happy that she was released from the shackles of her addiction. She once again had hope for change.

When our resistance to growth becomes stronger than the life-force energy we have moving forward, growth is no longer a viable option, and hope becomes a worn-out dream that in reality is nonexistent and only a possibility in the next incarnation.

OCD

The addictive nature drains our energy when it points toward gratification, since it is unsustainable and therefore continuously sought. A gratifying behavior that filled the gap from the movement of life may have brought comfort in a moment, but has turned into a prodigious compulsion.

When I was a child, the saying "If you step on a crack, you'll break your mother's back" was a silly, but catchy phrase. For me, I took silly to the extreme and was terrified to step on a crack. I didn't want to be responsible for breaking my mother's back, or I thought that was the reason. I had several such compulsions that I devotedly abided by, none of which had anything to do with the immaturity of being a child.

As an adult, before I could leave my house, I used to scan the stovetop, checking that all seven knobs were in the Off position. It didn't matter that I hadn't turned on the stove all morning. In my head I counted all seven knobs, like a teacher taking attendance, making sure all her students were present. I followed my compulsion long enough that if I left the house without the routine, my unconscious nagged at me about all the possibilities that could happen if I had indeed left the house with a burner lit.

At one time the habit began as a system to alleviate an uncomfortable empty space I needed to fill. Initially it must have been gratifying, as it gave the illusion of control, which in turn allowed me to feel safe momentarily, during what was probably an anxious state. Over time, it became a terribly inconvenient and annoying compulsion. To break the addictive habit that served no purpose, I had to leave and suffer the consequences of not checking the stove. My departure from home became synonymous with withdrawal, as my unconscious taunted me when I left without checking the stove. The inner turmoil was a battle of unconscious need against conscious logic, with my emotions cheering on the need. It went from "My home might burn down" to "That's why I have insurance," "My dog will die in the fire" to "The stove is not on. Relax." Finally I had to surrender to faith that everything would be okay, or not.

Sometimes the impulse to check the stove still tugs at me when I leave my home. It happens mostly when I am distracting myself with gratifying stuff and not spending enough time doing things that fulfill me. The addictive process of seeking gratification is a subtle betrayal to who we are, because it disperses our energy away from fulfilling our divine potential as an individual. The addictive nature pointed toward gratification is the black hole of consciousness.

Kill in God's Name

We can't forget the fanatic, in the same family as addiction. While fanaticism comes in many forms, like any addiction, it is bred from the addictive nature, where energy is misdirected. The fanatic pours his energy into a cause at the exclusion of all else. Sometimes it excludes base values. A woman in dog rescue was supporting a lofty cause until she ended up hording more than fifty animals, before the local animal shelter was alerted. Three-fourths of the fifty were dehydrated and had severe malnutrition. The other one-forth required invasive medical care or were beyond treatment and were immediately euthanized.

In some cases, whatever or whoever conflicts with the fanatic must be verbally or physically annihilated. For example, it is not uncommon for a fanatic to kill in the name of God. It may appear the fanatic is fighting a cause for the masses, but his battle, under the guise of good, is a shield that protects him from anything that threatens his security. Such threats might be the movement of life in the form of change. Fanaticism is devotion upside down, pointing toward gratification rather than a testament of faith, even if the fanatic parrots religious scripture. If our energy is not circulating back to our Spirit, divinity is not communicated in our actions.

Divine Discontent

An ancient Hindu fable goes something like this: An old woman was frantically searching all around the area outside her home. A man passing by witnessed her despair, felt sorry for her, and offered help. He asked, "What are you looking for, ma'am? Let me help you."

She replied, "I lost my sewing needle. It was my favorite one. Thank you for helping me; you are a dear."

Time went by, and neither person seemed closer to finding the needle, after scouring the area several times. Becoming impatient with the seemingly futile search, the man said, "Ma'am, we have searched all over. Do you know about where you were the last time you had your beloved needle?"

She replied, "Yes, of course, I had it at my sewing table, in my sewing room." She pointed to a window in her house.

He was perplexed. "Ma'am, why are we looking out here, then?"

Her startling answer was, "Isn't that what most people do? Aren't we supposed to look outside for what we have misplaced inside?"

We seek fulfillment in life, but trade it out for gratification, because gratification is the seasoning of our senses. Before we know it, gratification is the flavor we can't live without. The momentary and fleeting comfort of something else becomes more important than the permanent and long-lasting fulfillment found in connecting with ourselves. We become addicted to filling an empty space with life rather than filling our life.

Filling our life is not about a schedule filled in with events, people, and places of interest, but about connecting to ourselves. We cannot purposely fill our life, if we don't spend time daily connecting with who we are. Ask questions such as, "What am I feeling?" "Why do I feel that way?" "What did that mean to me?" By asking such questions, we slowly begin to direct our energy inward rather than away from ourselves. When we know who we are, we are subject to synchronistic occurrences that draw to us the events, people, and activities that fulfill us.

The irony is that life is not meant to bring us comfort. Fulfillment always has an edge of discomfort. Divine discontent pushes us forward to keep pace with the movement of life. There was a period in my life when I felt balanced and connected to myself. Looking back, it was a brief period in time I have failed to recapture. What I have learned is balance is not the embodiment of growth, but a sparingly allotted pause, like a vacation. If we hold ourselves separate from the meaningless and mundane aspects of life, those things that cause irritation and disorder, we are denied the glory of growth. By constantly striving to find meaning in life, amid daily living, we are given the opportunity to deepen our connection with ourselves.

Strength is not developed by enduring life's hardships, but from the inner connection made as a result of hardship. Connecting with ourselves, we are the mustard seed that moves the mountain. Through that inner connection, all the levels we exist on are in sync. No energy is wasted fighting ourselves, and life has meaning, because we are living our potential.

Life is defined by the journey we walk each and every day. On that journey, when the shoes fit, I encourage you to take them off and walk barefoot, as you let go of the fears that bind you and be free to discover who you really are.

CPSIA information can be obtained at www.ICGtesting.com
Printed in the USA
LVOW130341200513

334458LV00001B/10/P

9 780985 640903